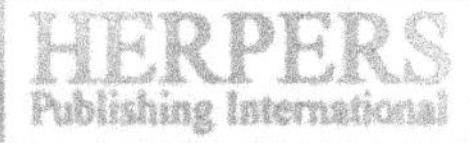
HERPERS
Publishing International

A CIP catalogue record for this book is available from the German Library.
(http://dnb.d-nb.de)

Copyright © 2016 Herpers Publishing International
www.herperspublishing.com
www.practice-drawing.com

ISBN: 978-3-946411-36-9

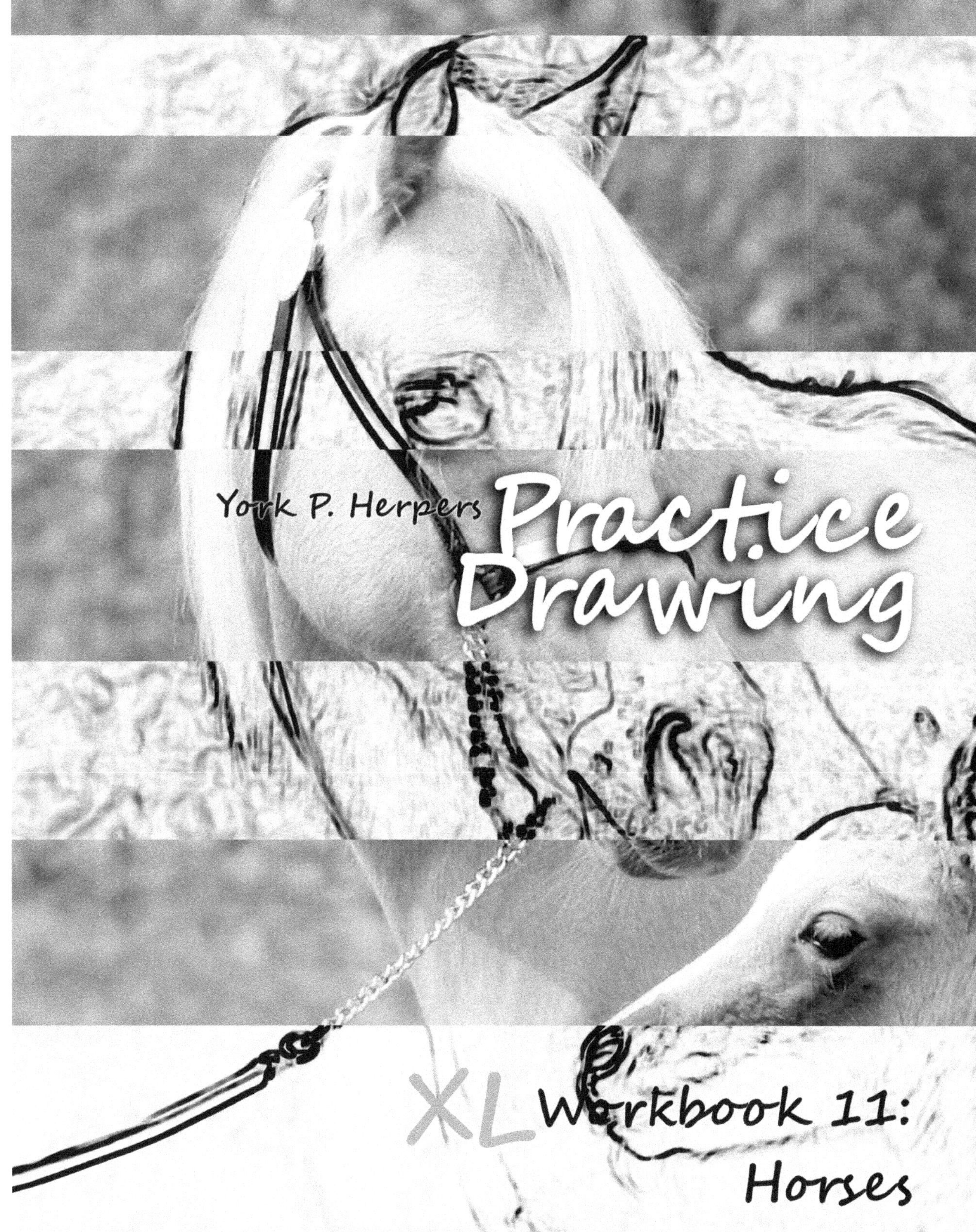

York P. Herpers
Practice Drawing
XL Workbook 11:
Horses
HERPERS
Publishing International

Freehand drawing – made easy!

Even in a digital world, freehand sketching is still a **recipe for success** for impressive works of art. It is **your own hand** that makes your art **unique**. Many people don't know their ability to draw. But even **unpracticed** line drawings can make for impressive images. It is actually the **imperfection** that turns your images into works of art.

This exercise book makes you an artist

Tracing is a simple and **proven method** to learn freehand drawing. After your exercises in this book, you will also succeed without templates because you will have developed a **sense of proportion and contours**.

The result: **impressive drawings that you have made yourself, even on the first attempt**.
These are **originals** that you should even **sign with your own name**. It is your hand that has created this remarkable work of art.

The **beautiful motifs** are what make each stroke of the pen or pencil pure joy.

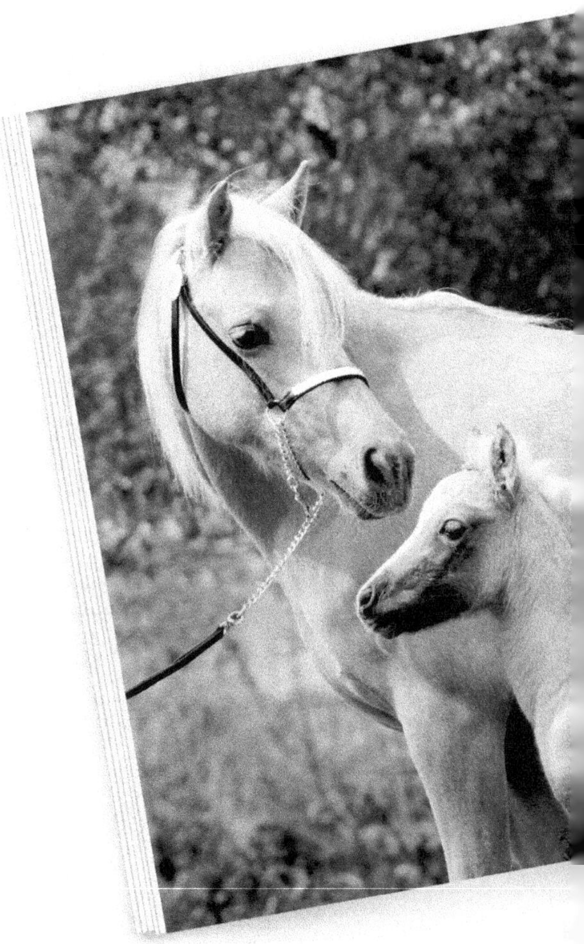

Take advantage of every free space to let your creativity run wild

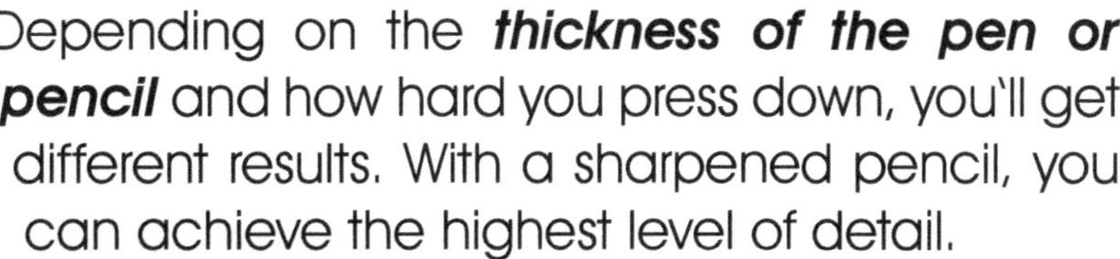

Depending on the **thickness of the pen or pencil** and how hard you press down, you'll get different results. With a sharpened pencil, you can achieve the highest level of detail.

With **wax pencils**, colored pencils, or crayons you can color your drawing or just add color effects.

With **charcoal pencils**, you can create rough drawings where it can be difficult to outline details, but can be just as artful.

You'll find **each motif twice** as an original template: one for trial and error and the second for your next draft.

Use the **rear of the sketch template** to create practice **tracing** or **shading** on the mirror image of the template.

The paperback format is handy and easy to take with you wherever you go, that way you can use any free moment to practise.

Explore this book and get stuck in:

It's simply fun!

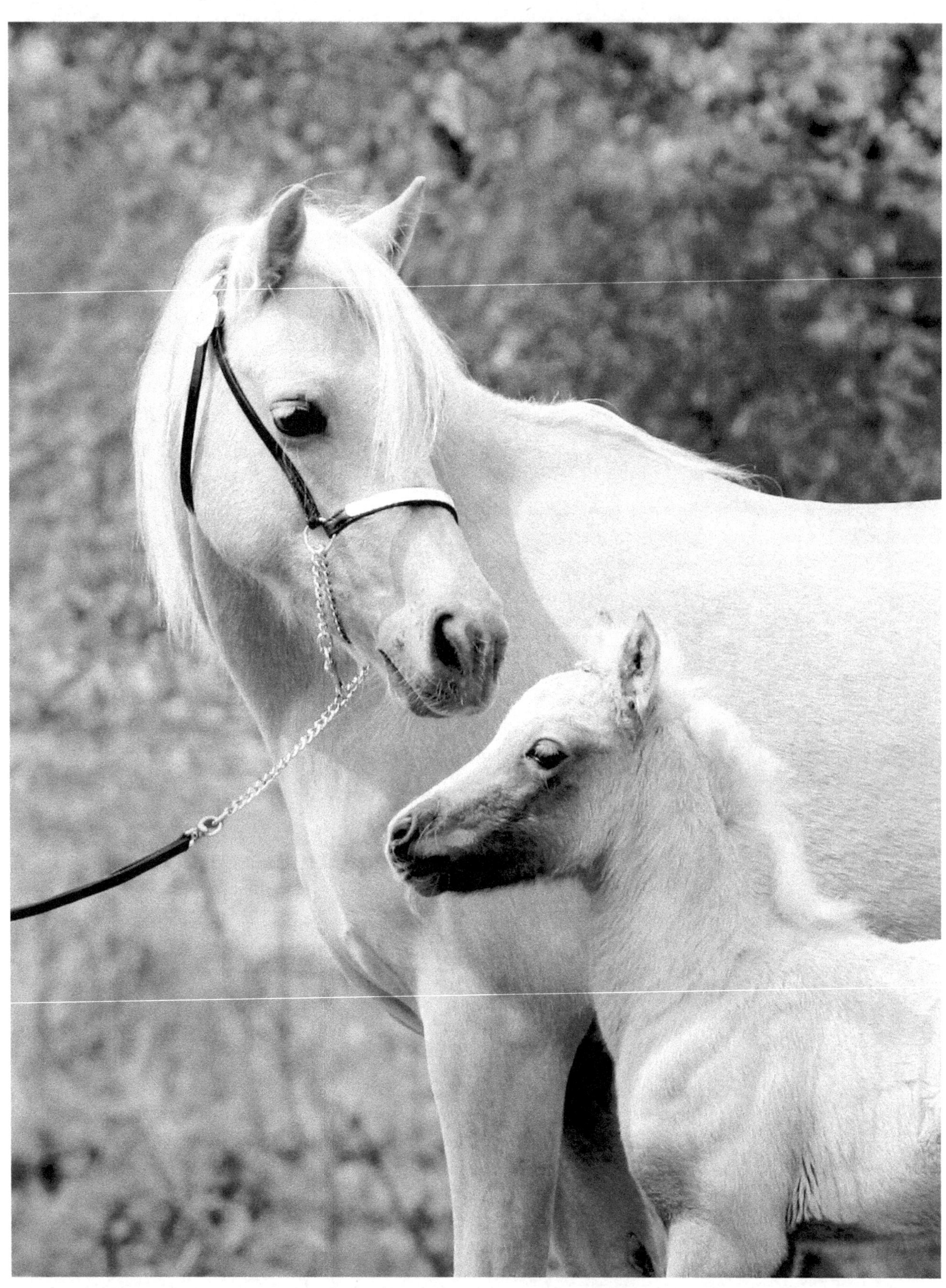

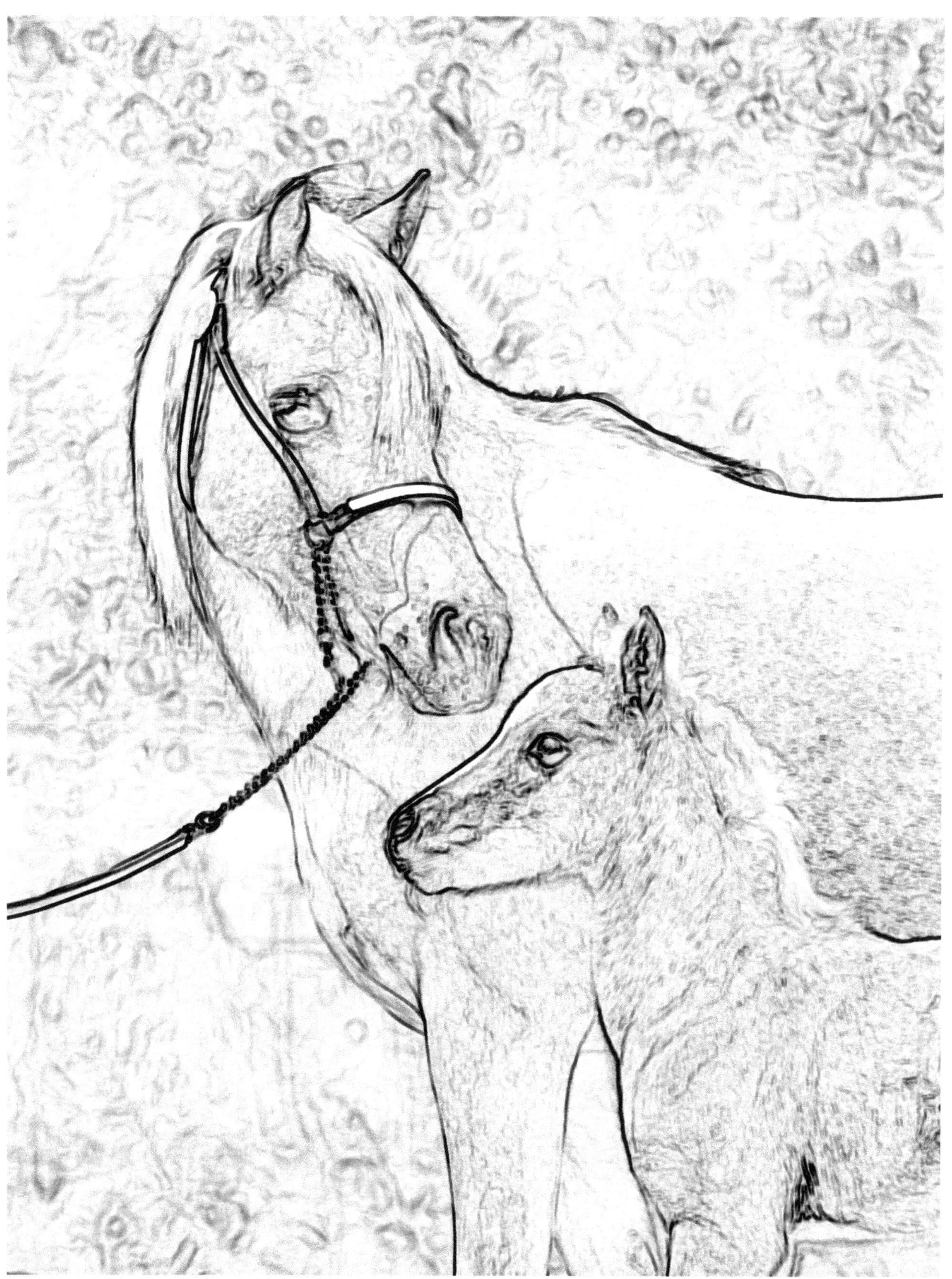

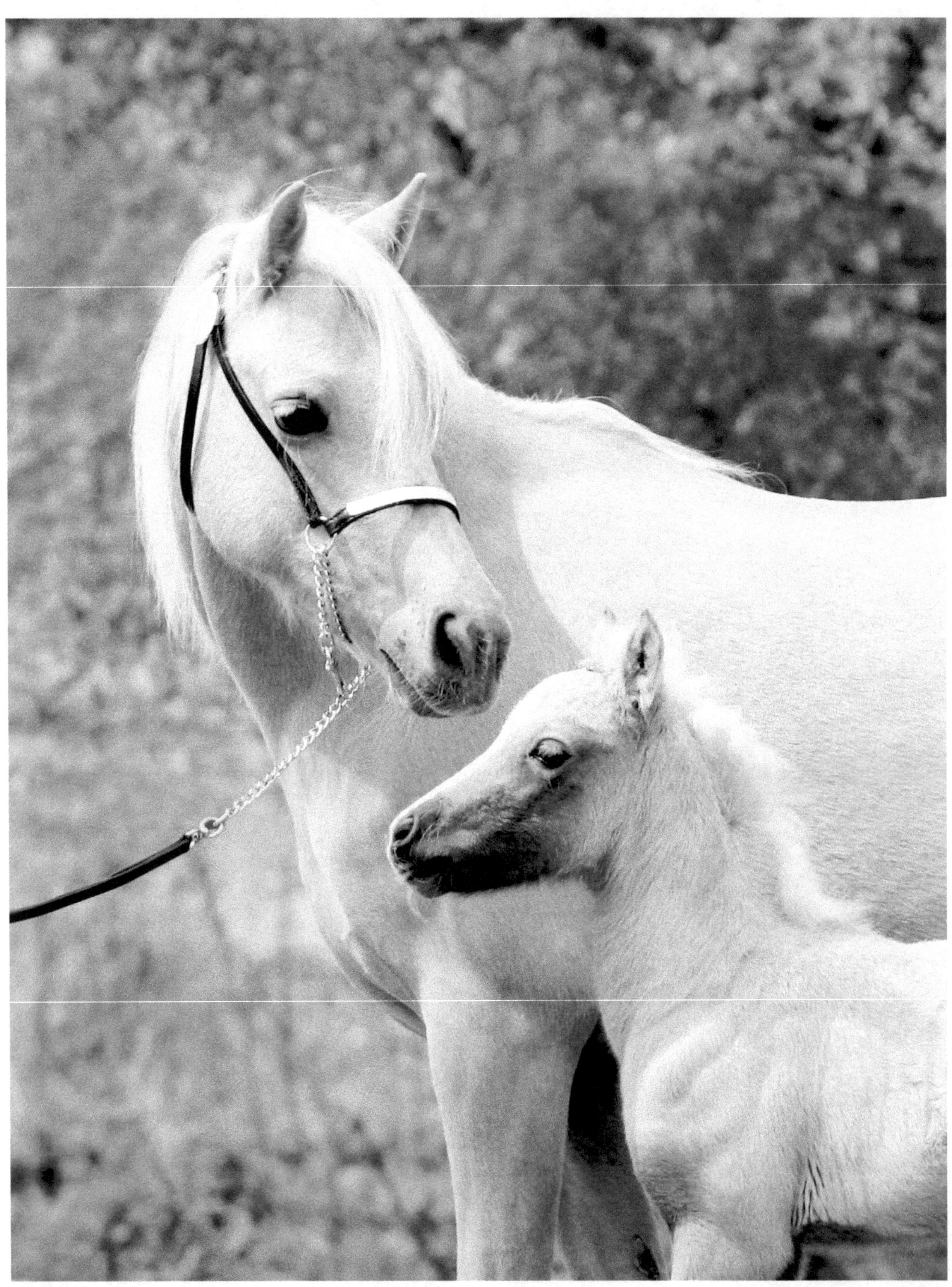

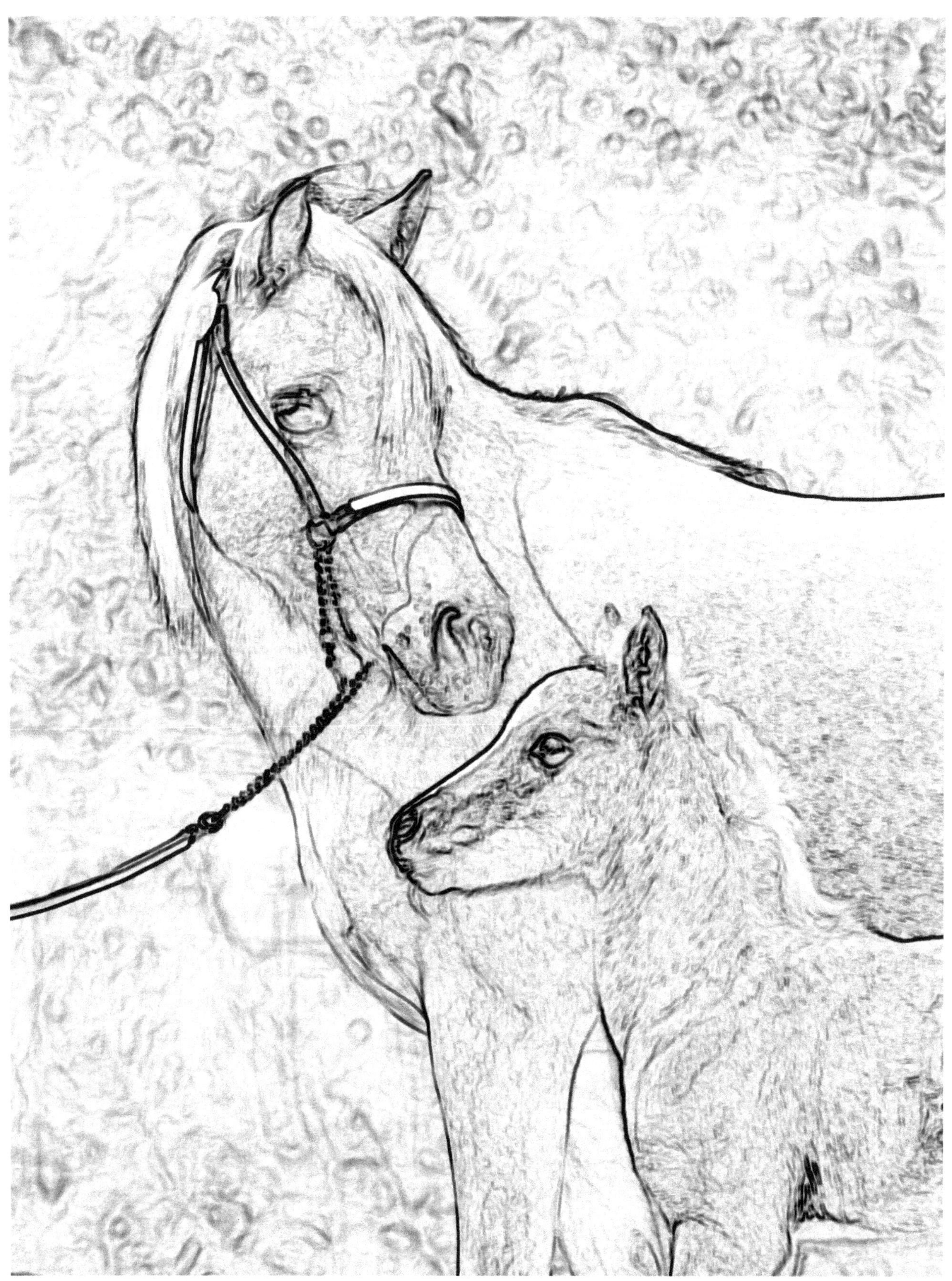

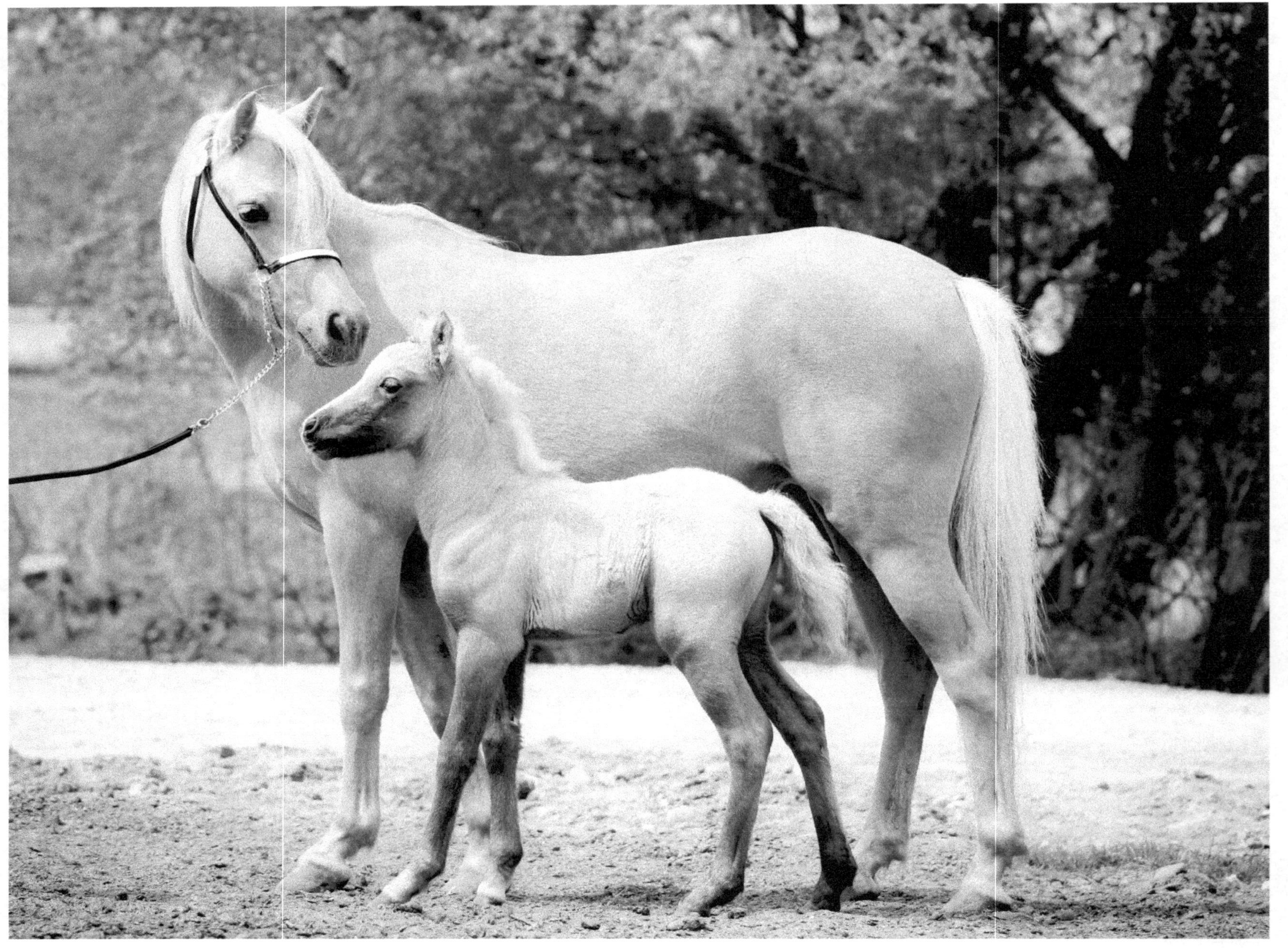

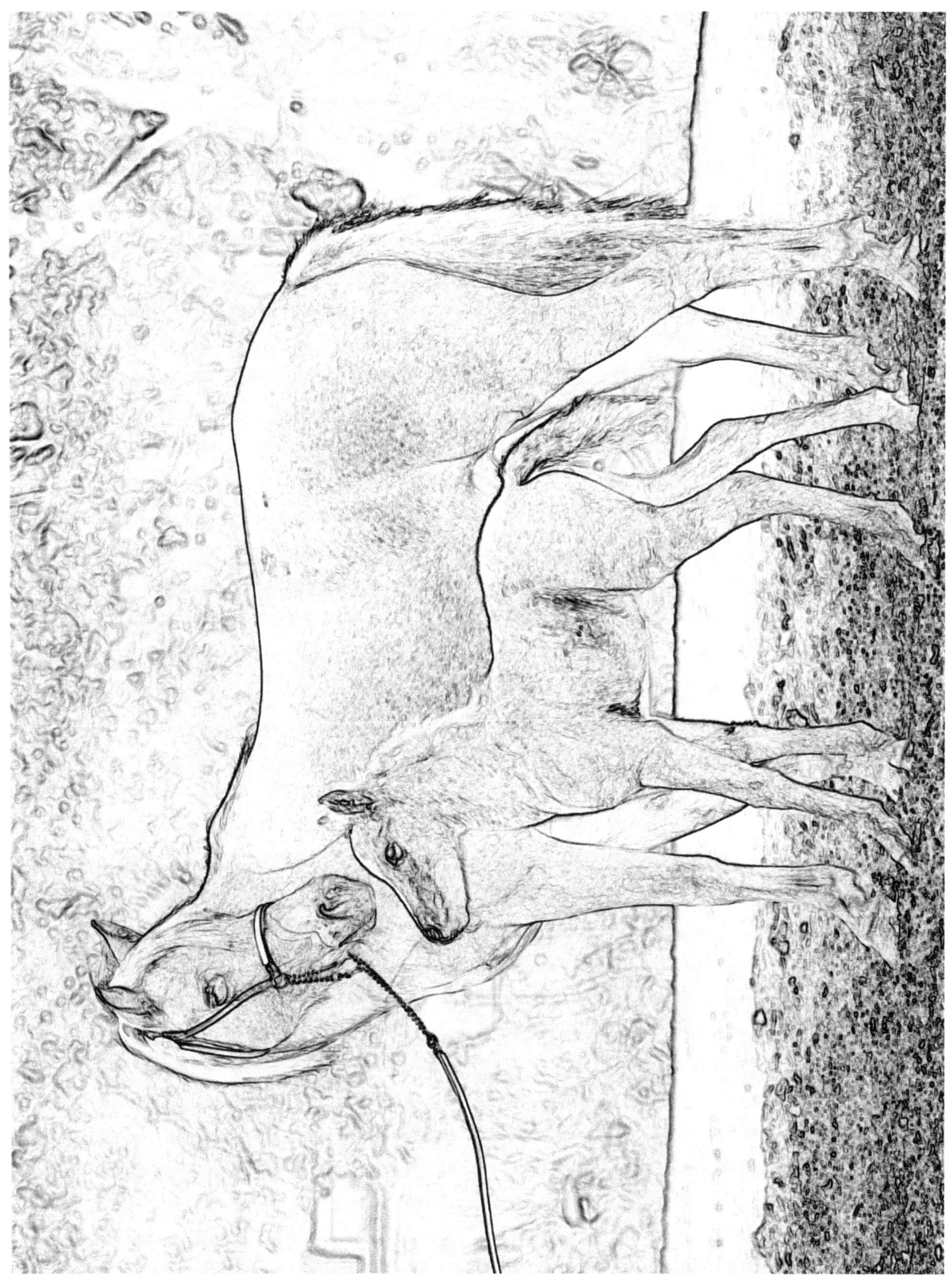

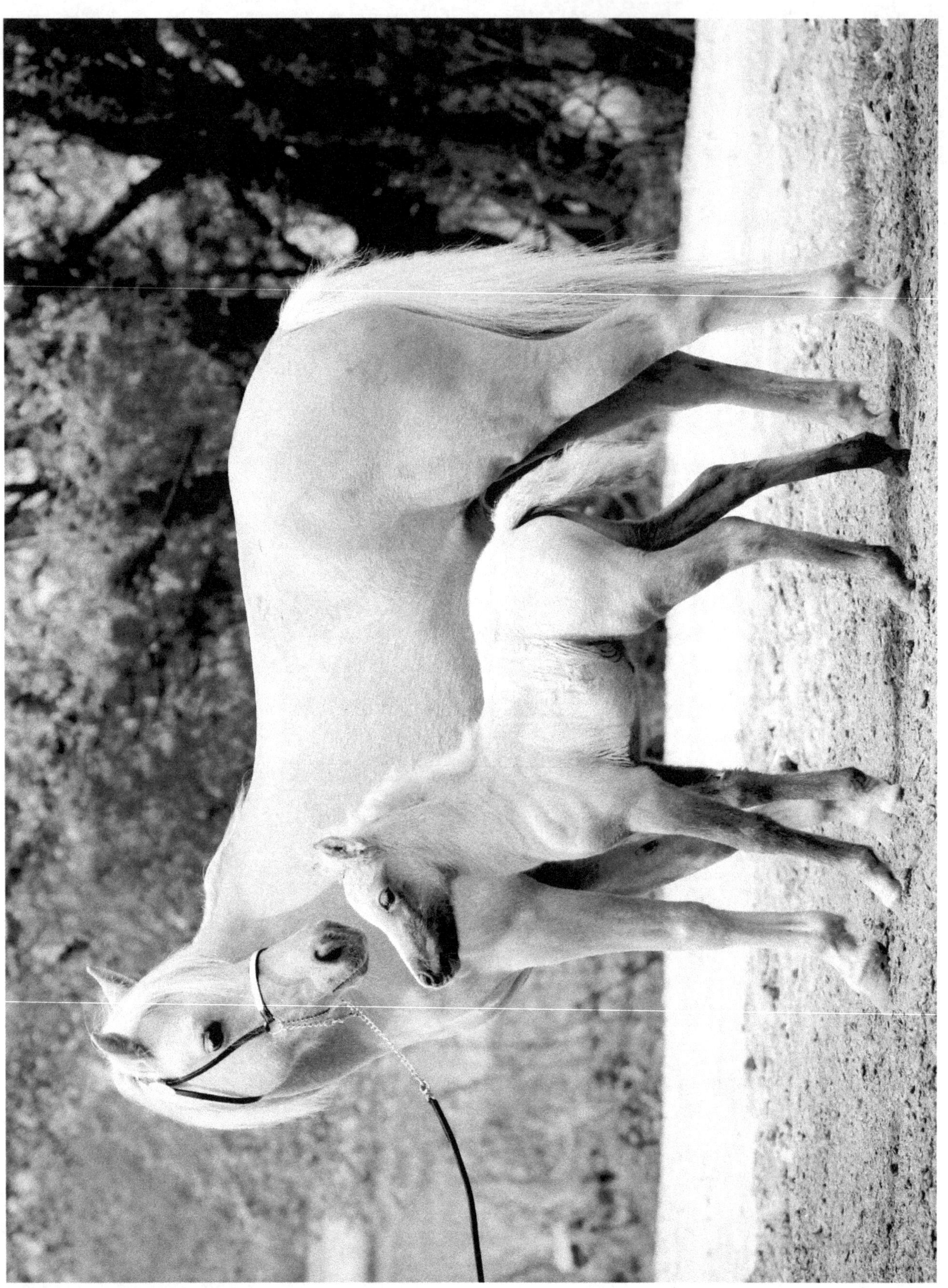

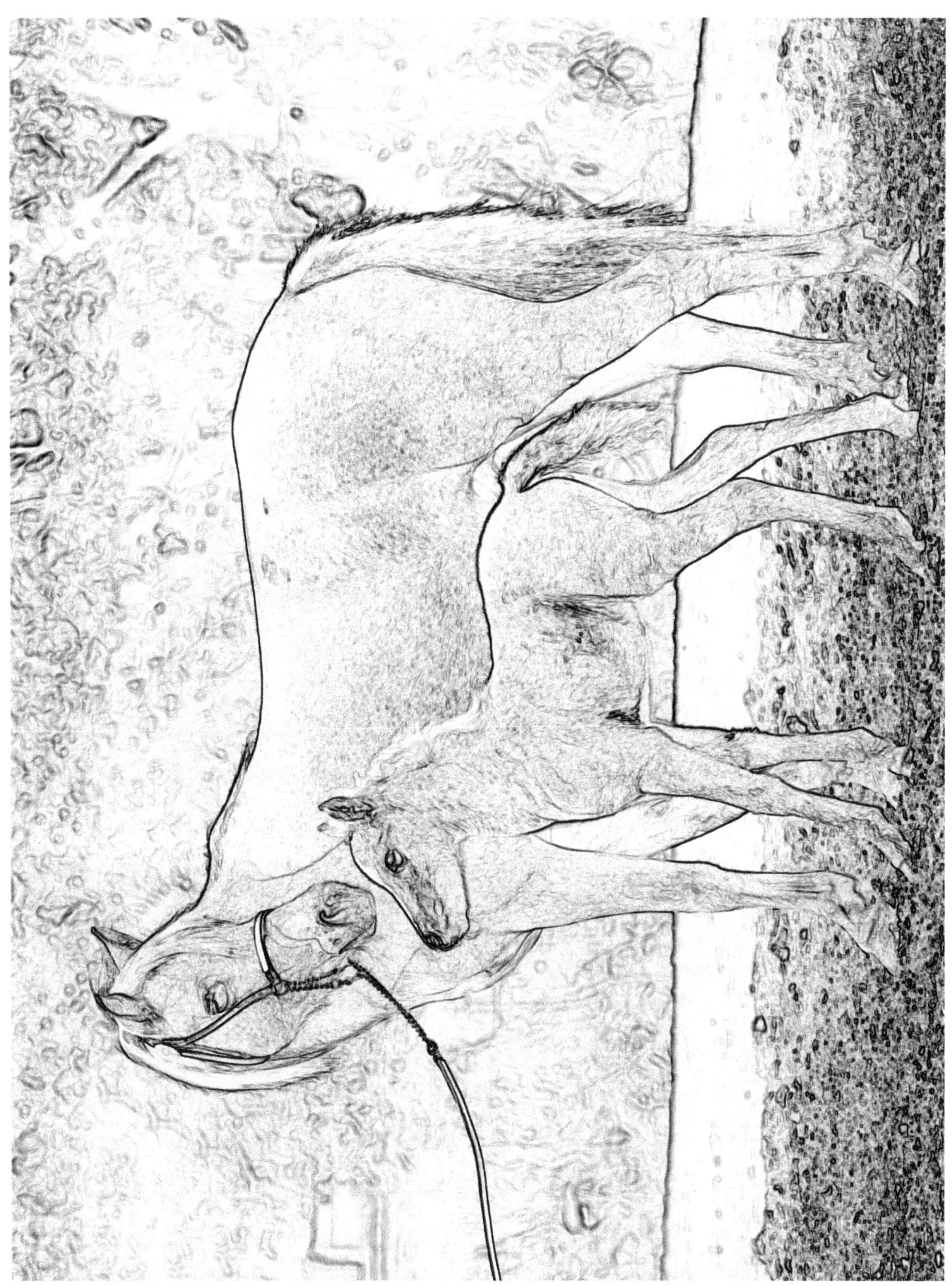

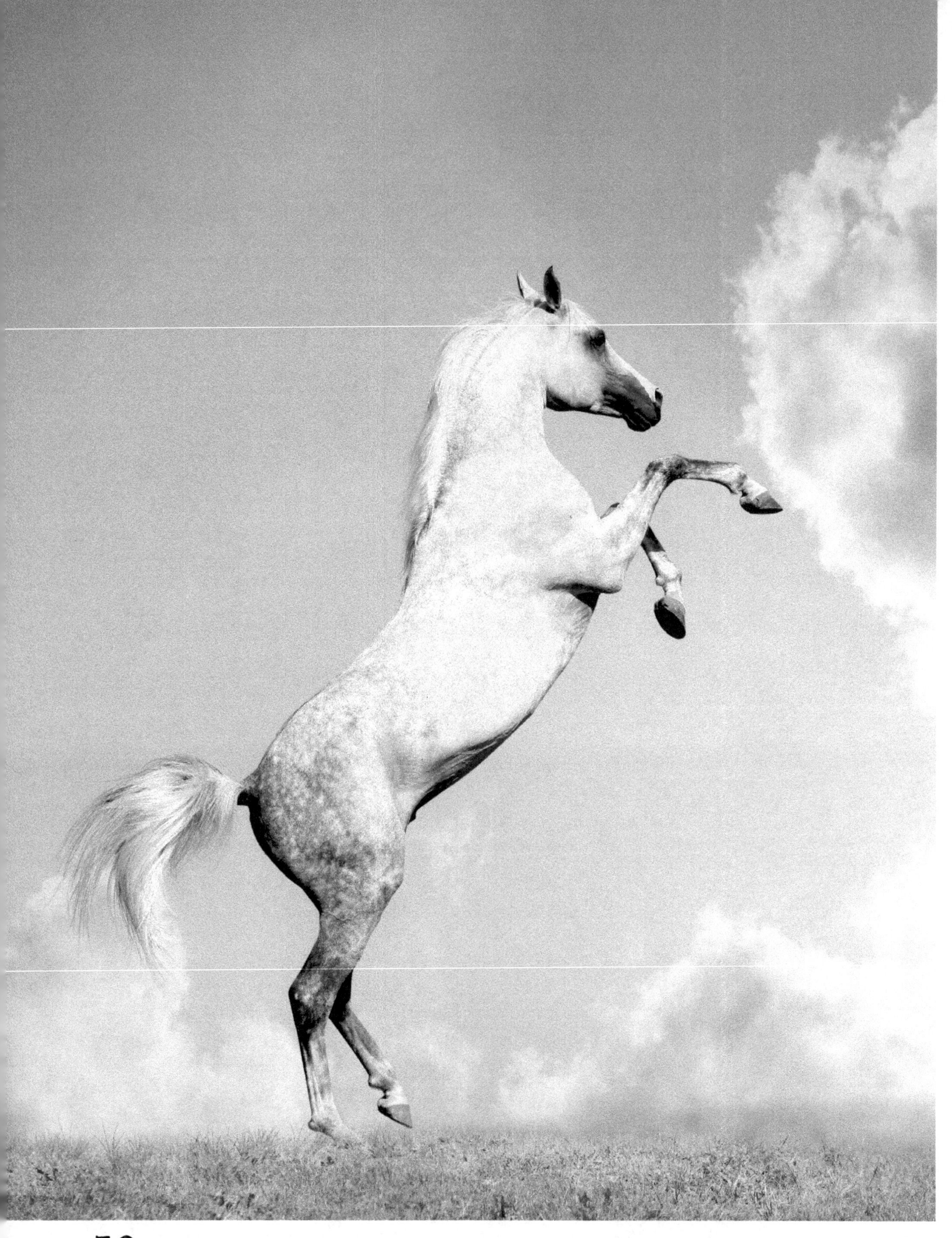

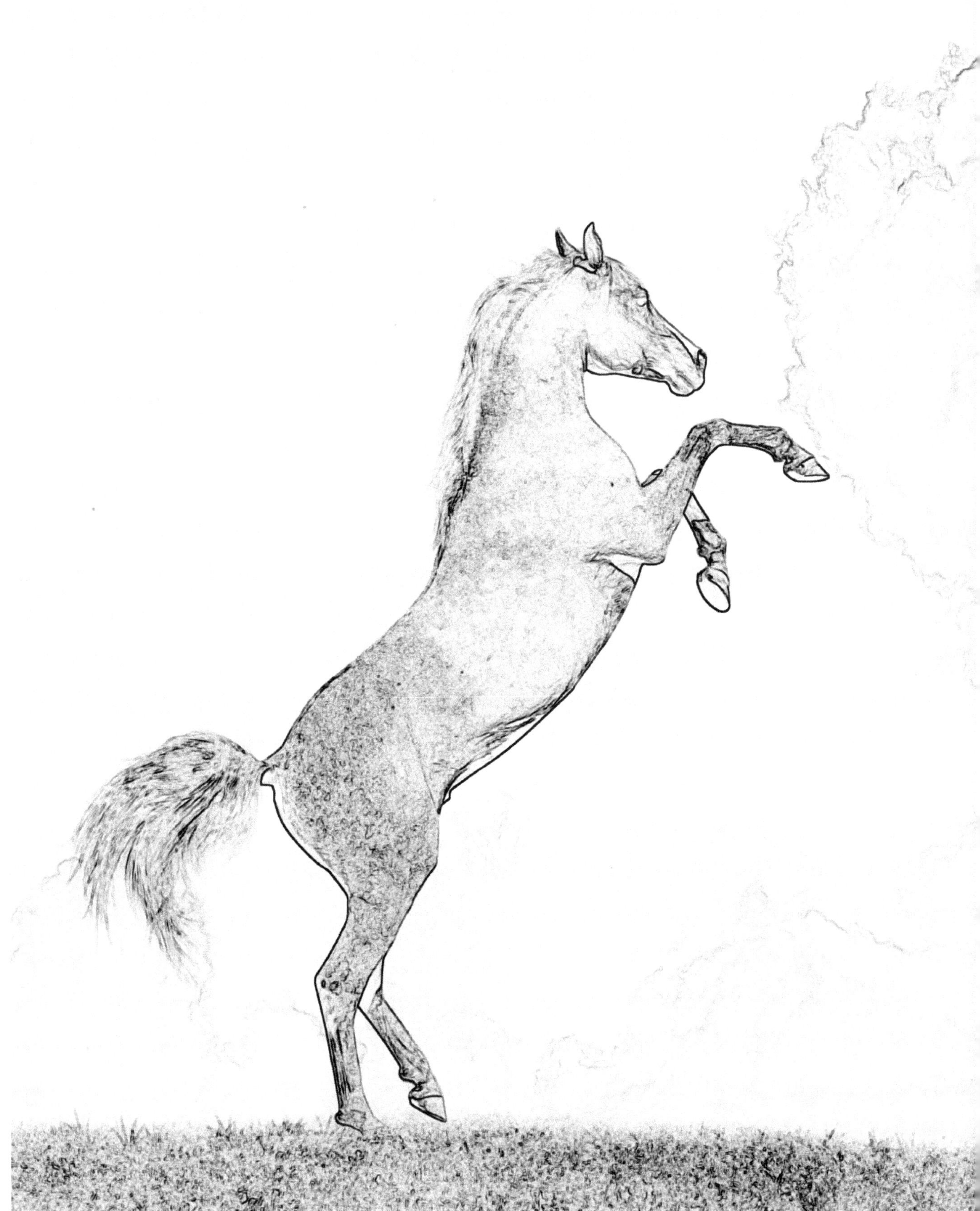

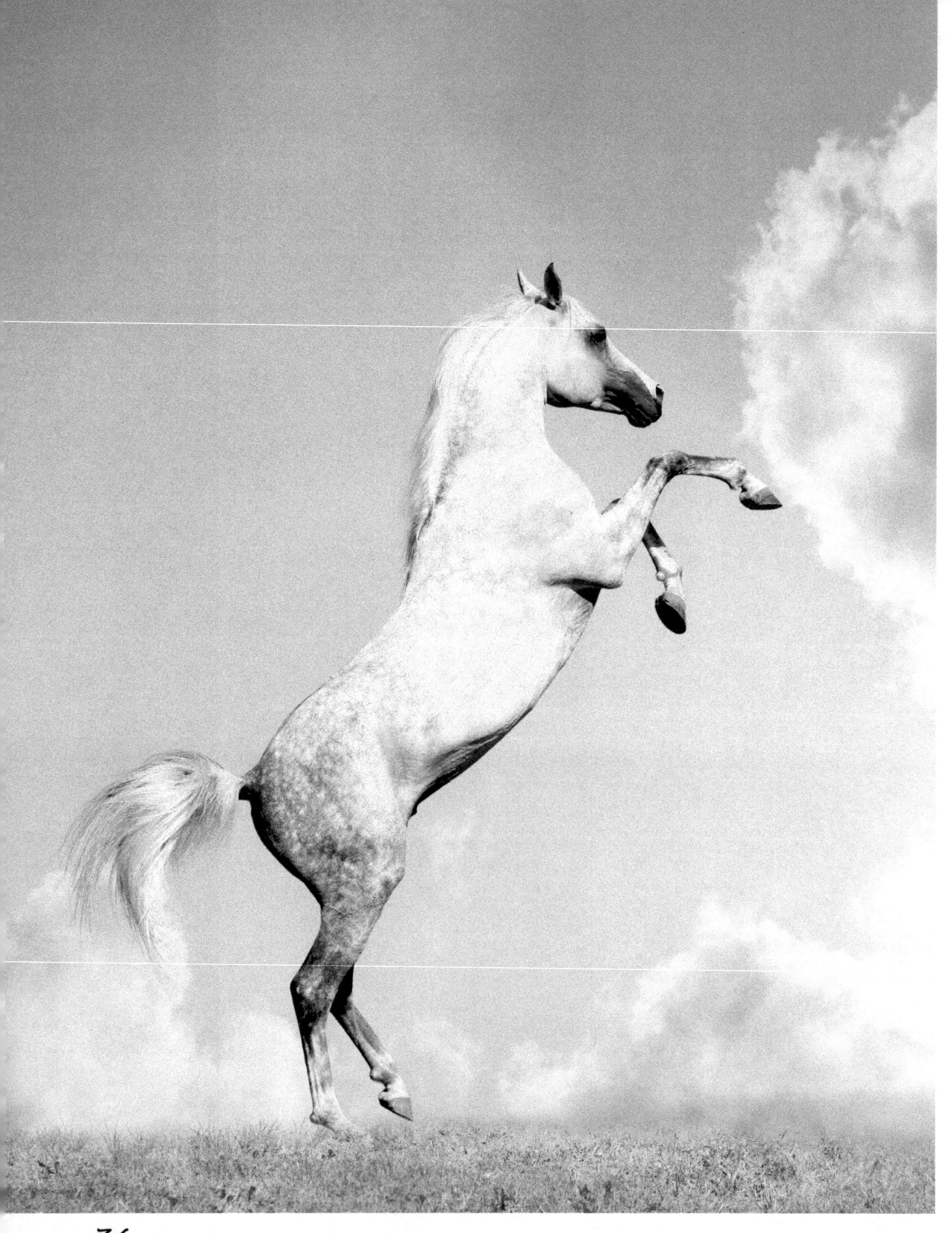

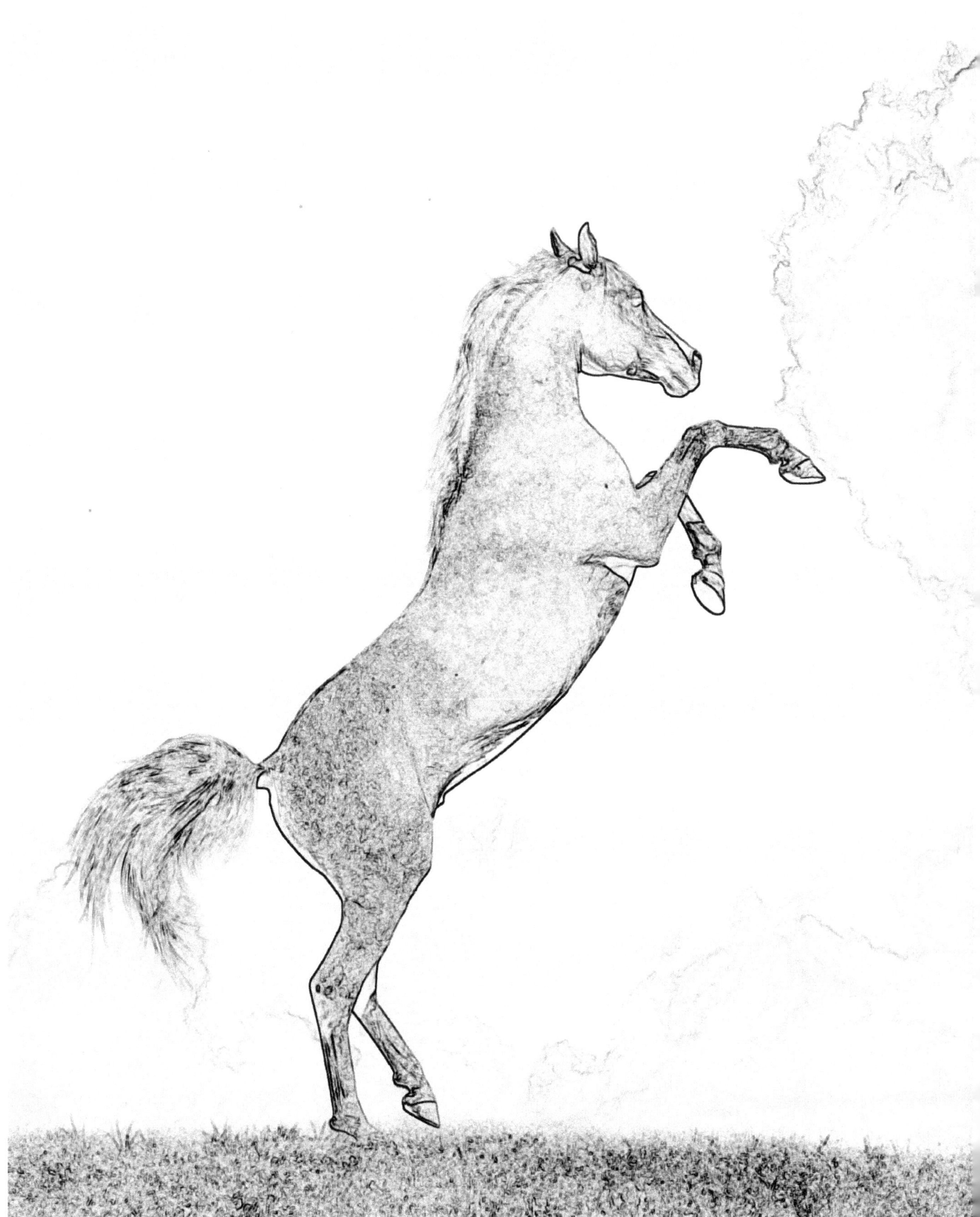

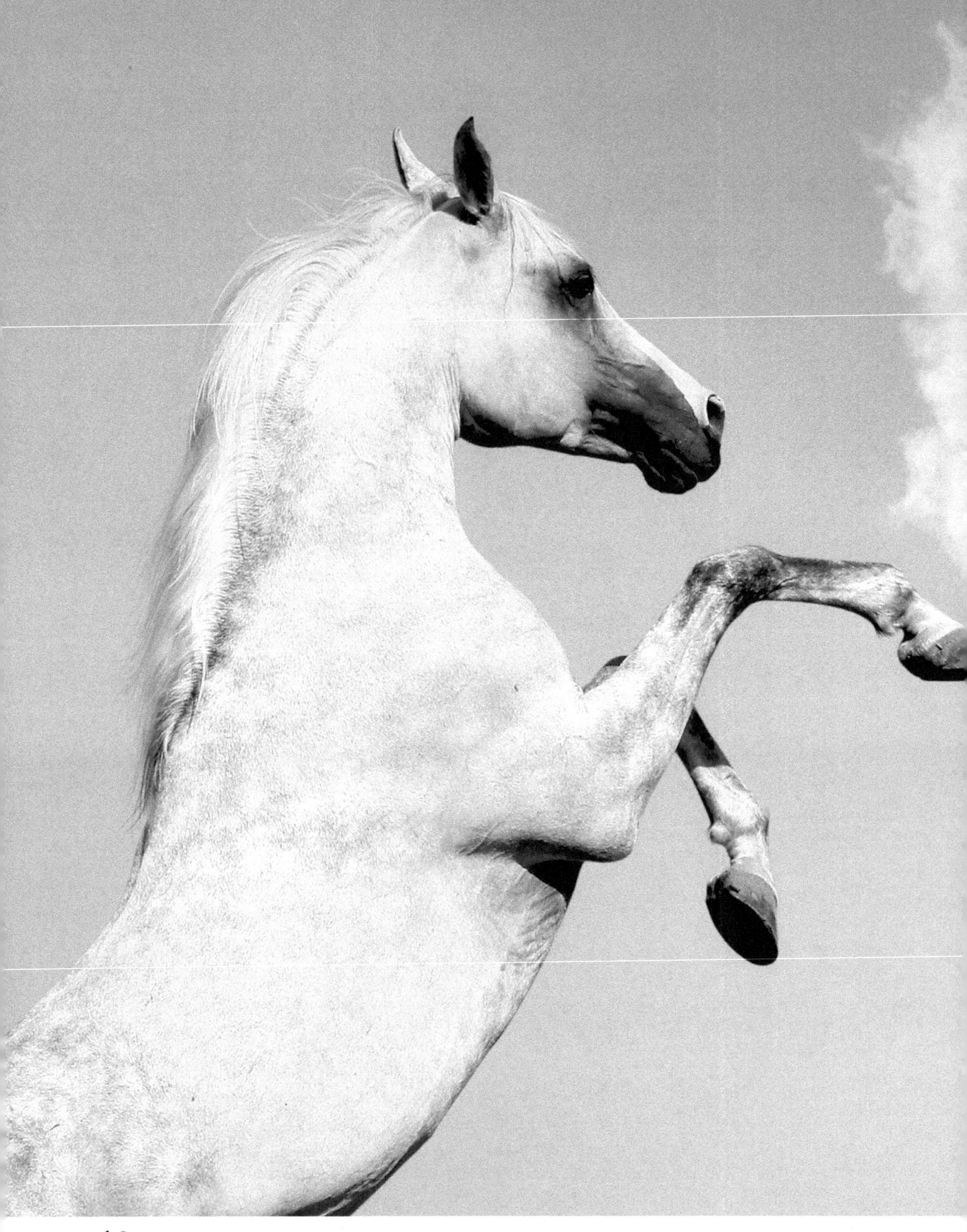

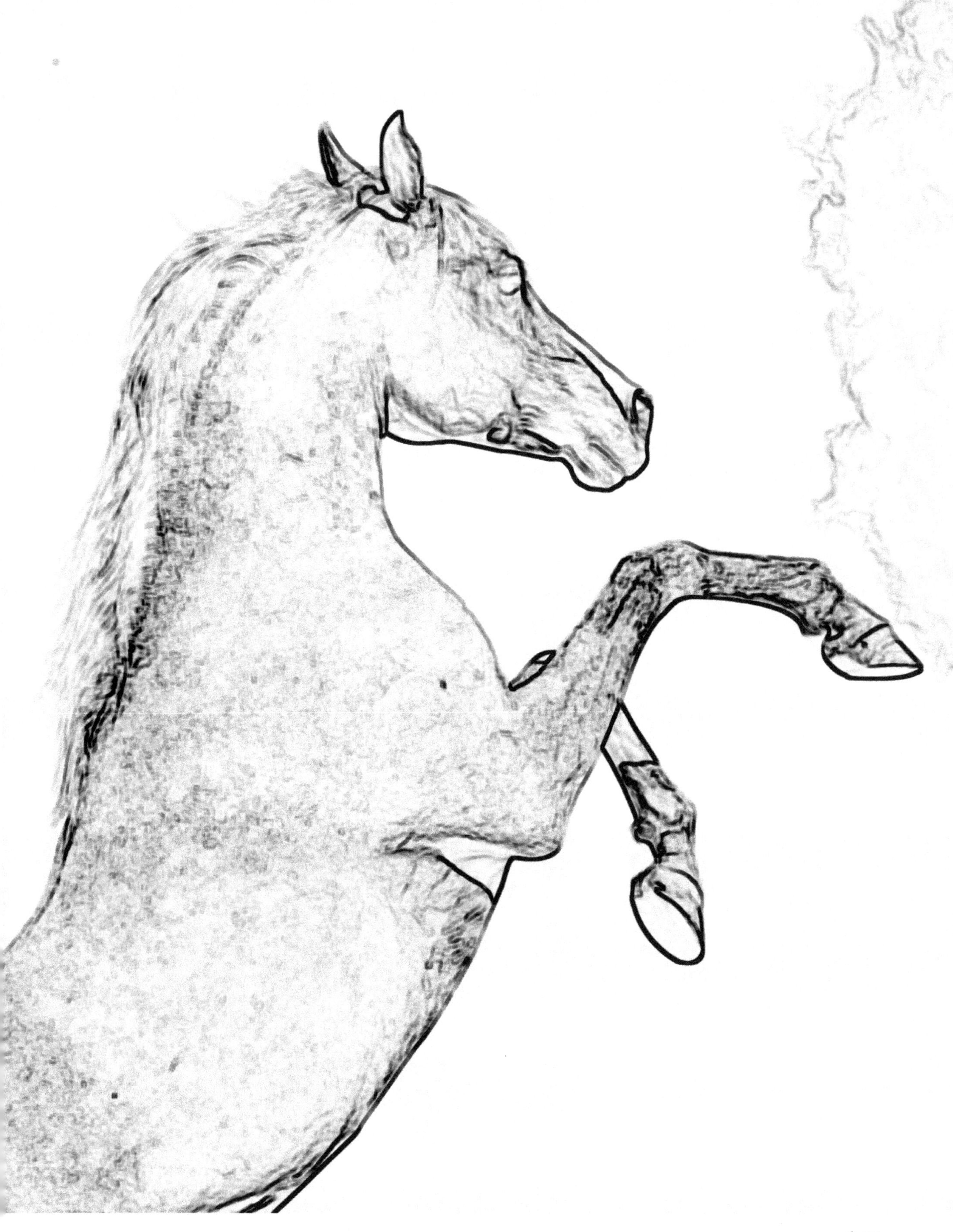

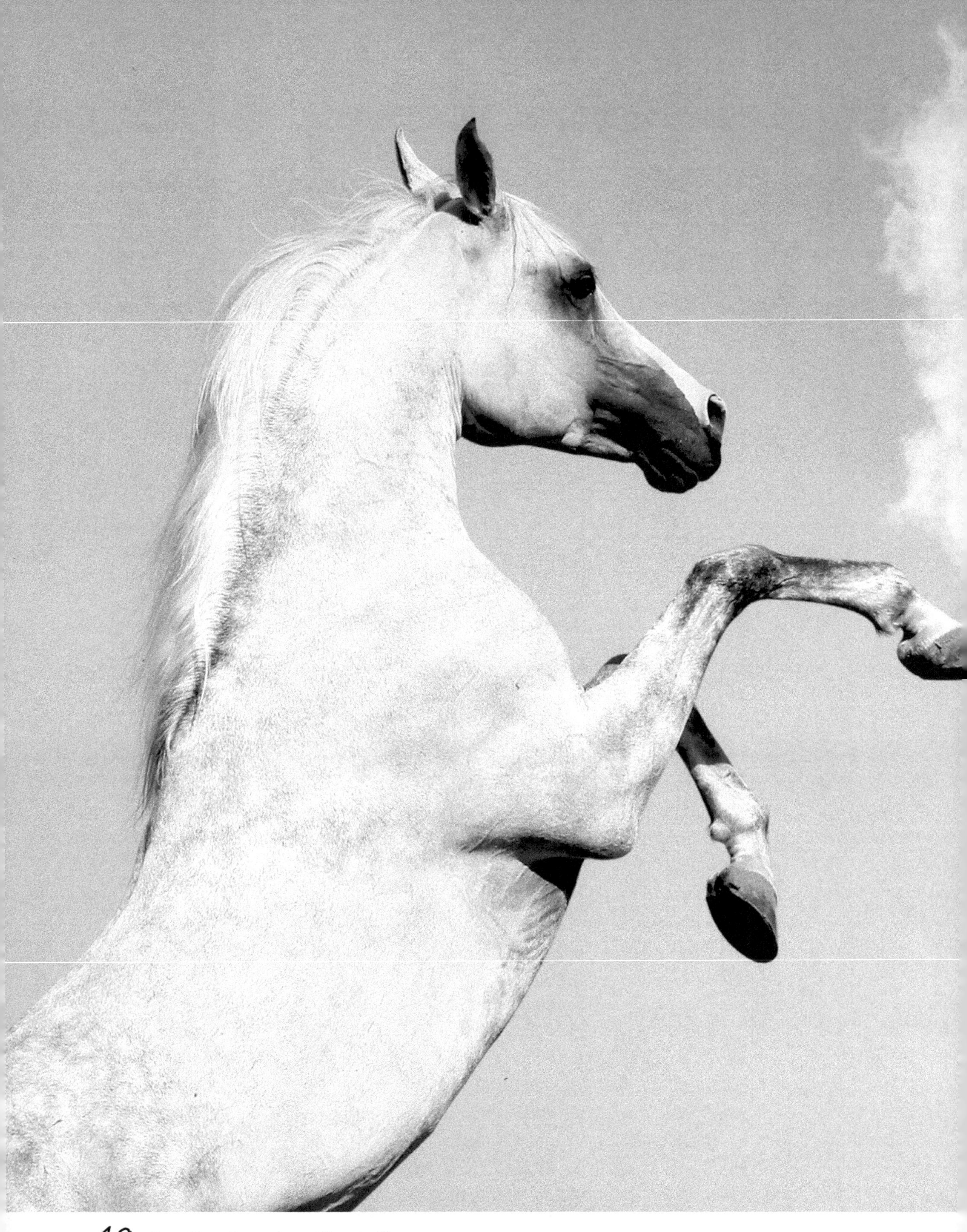

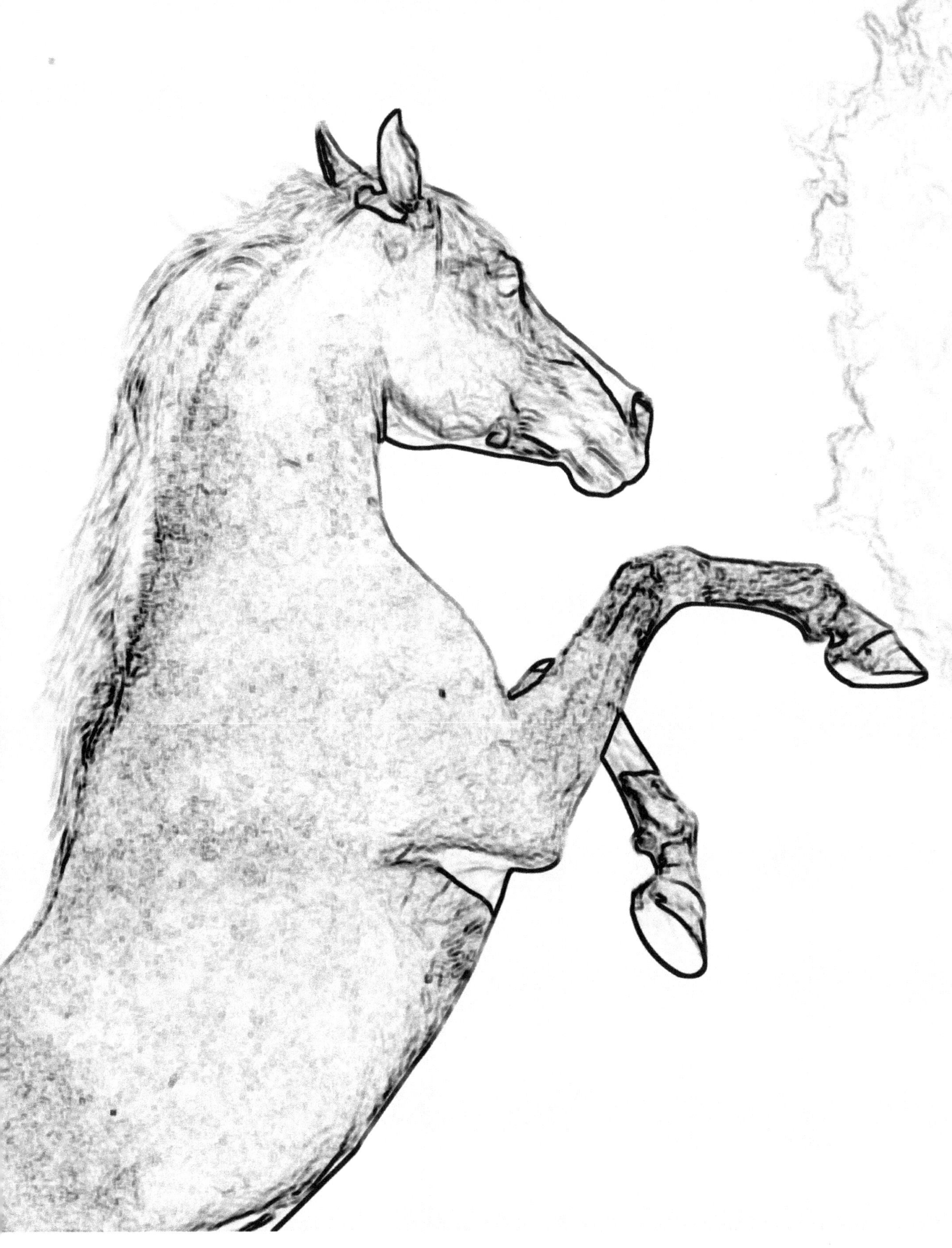

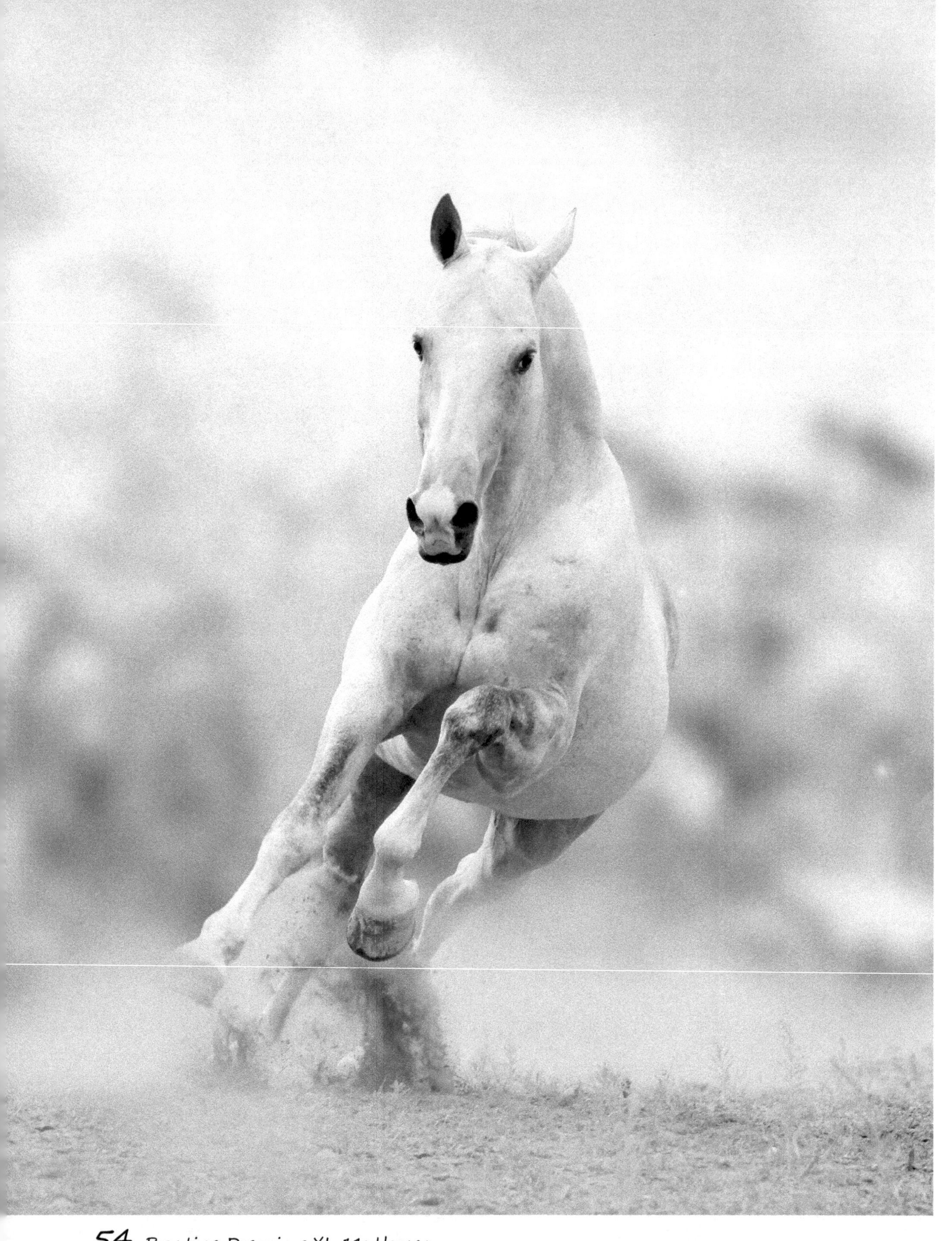

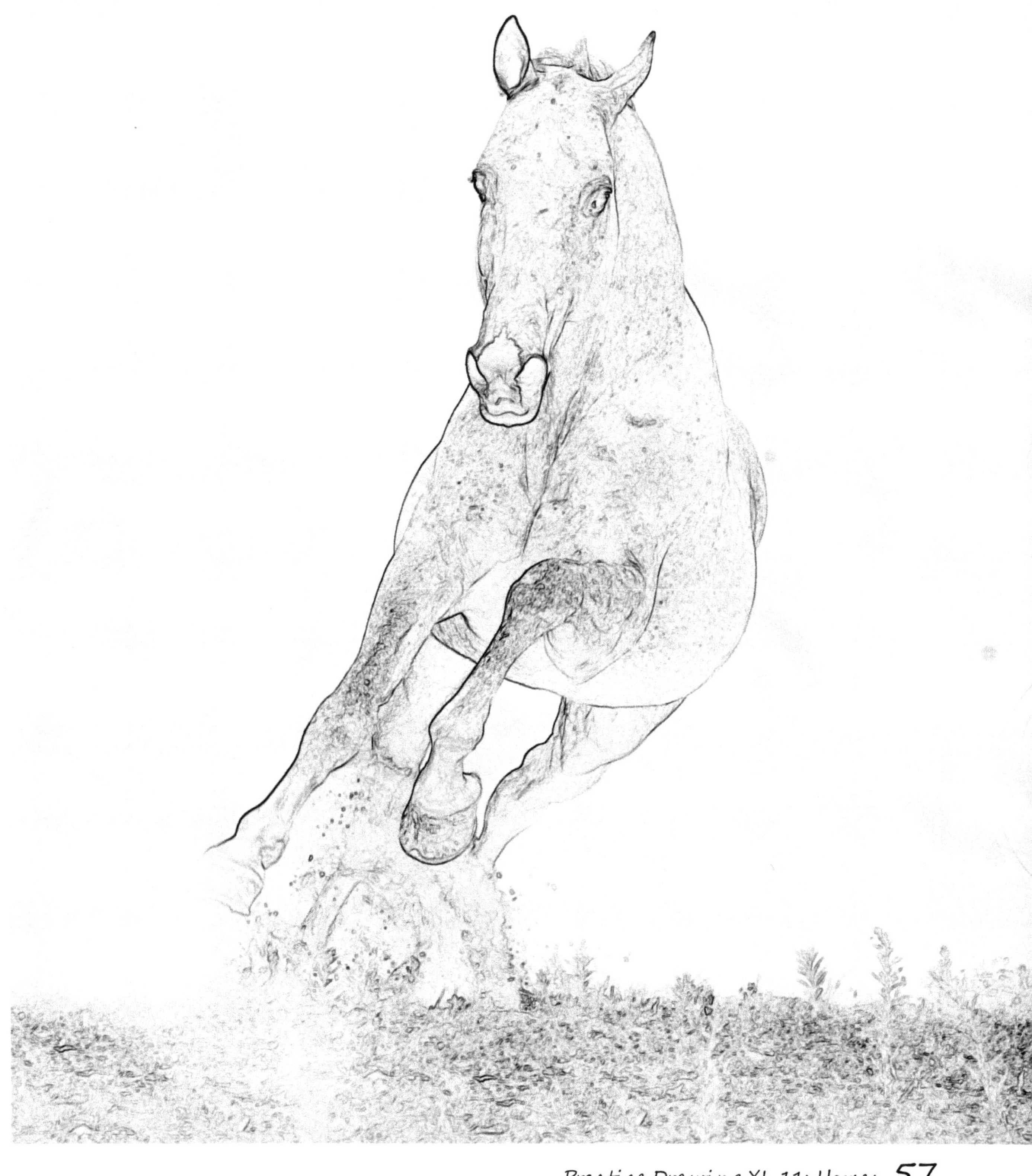

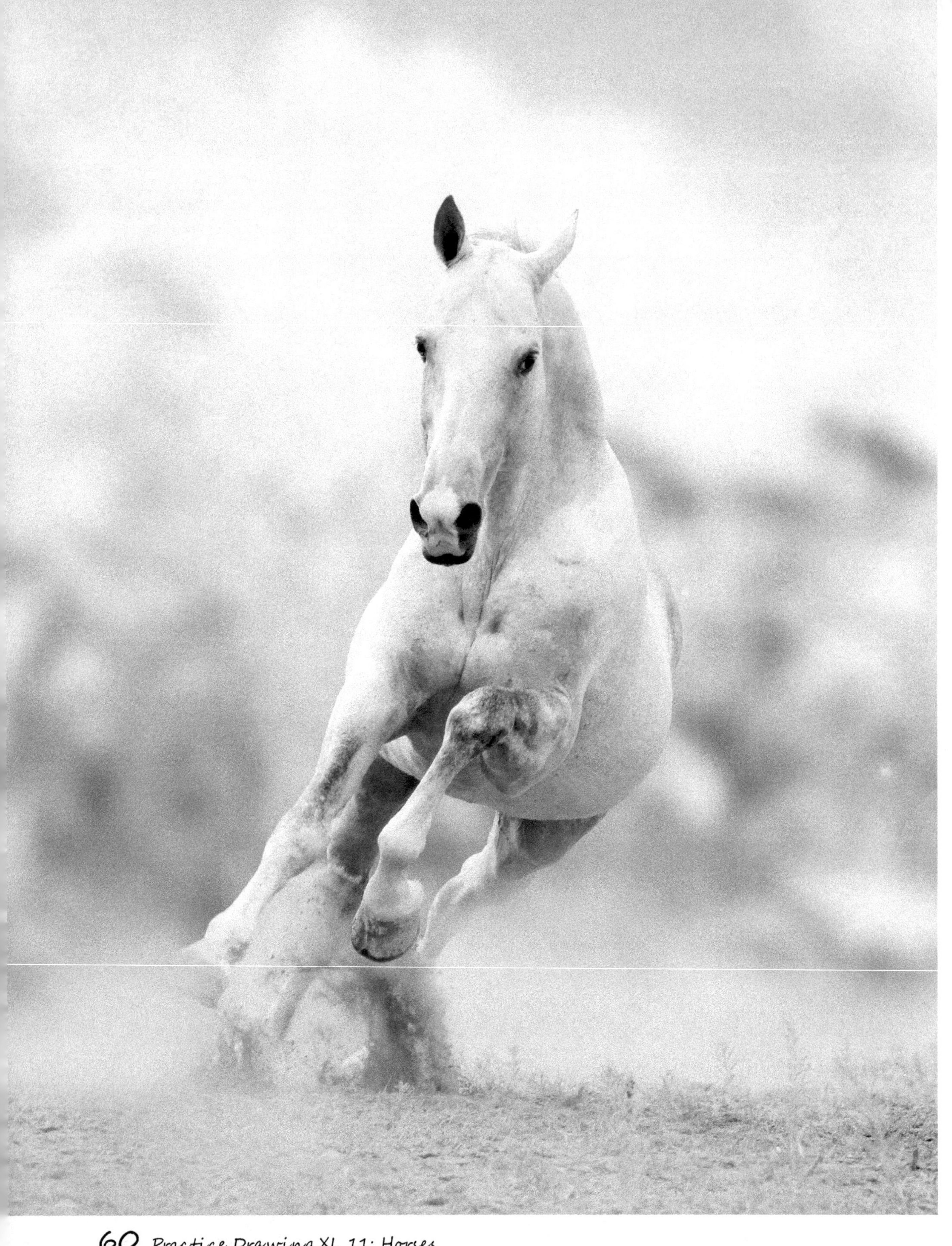

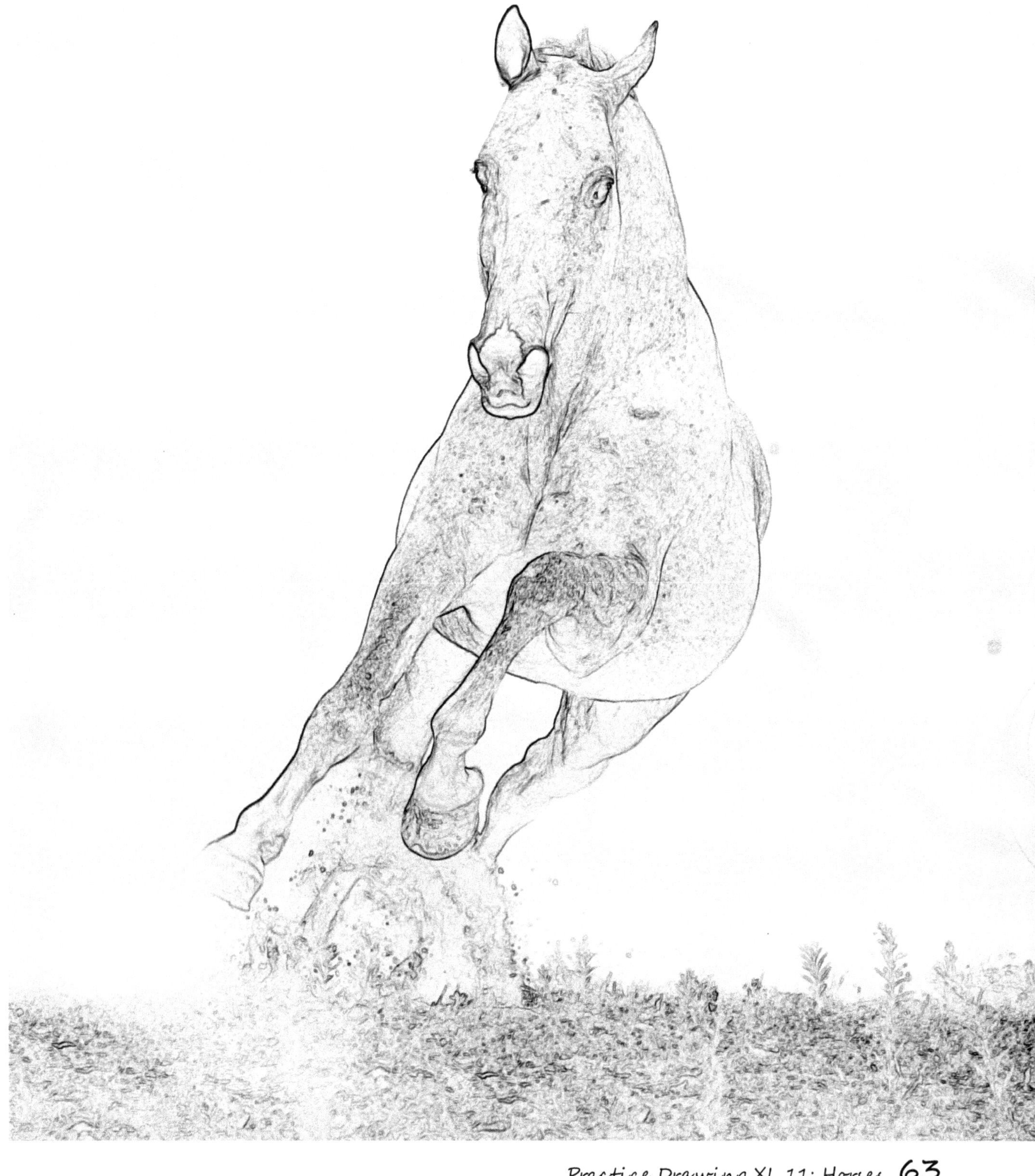

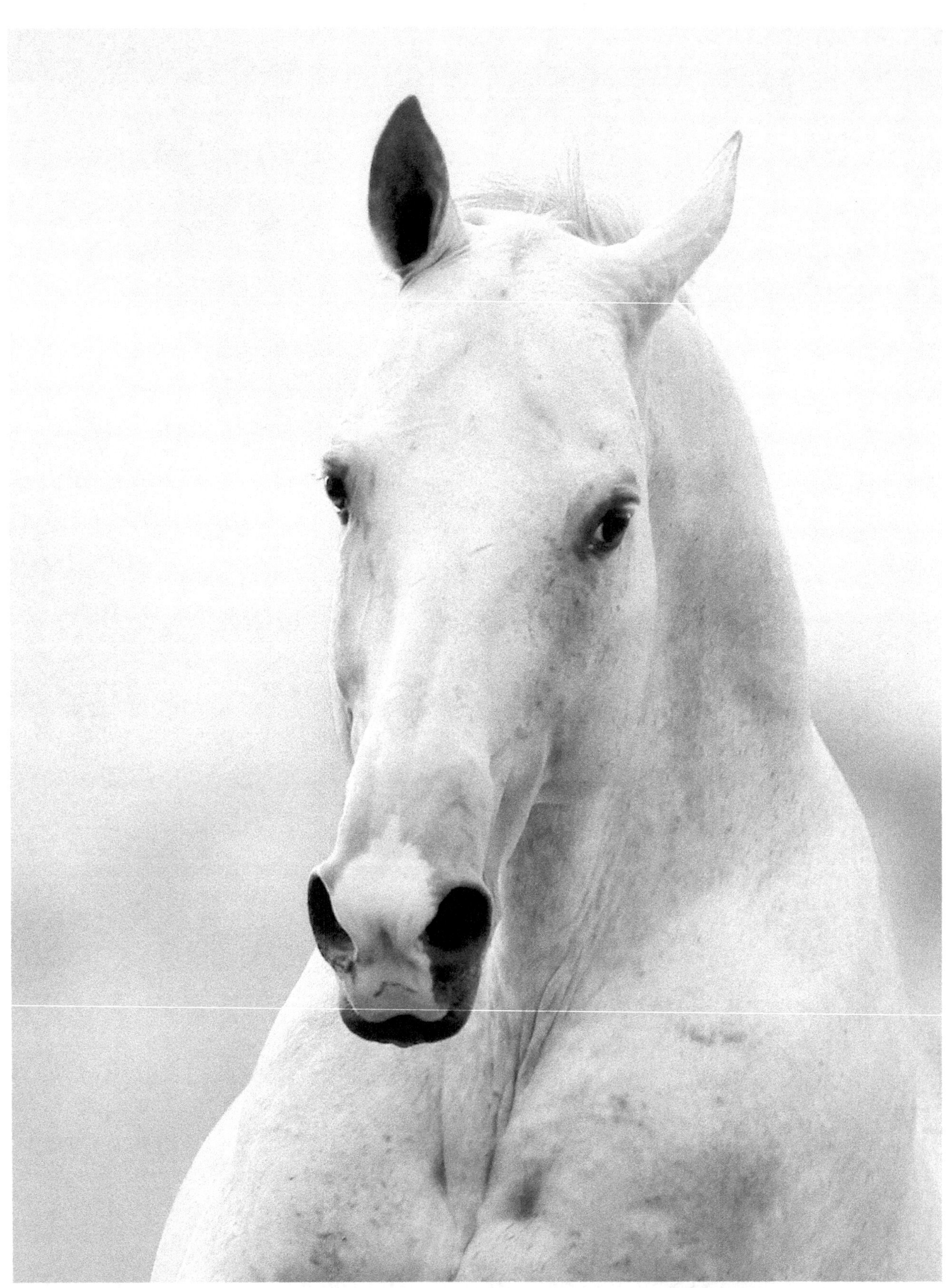

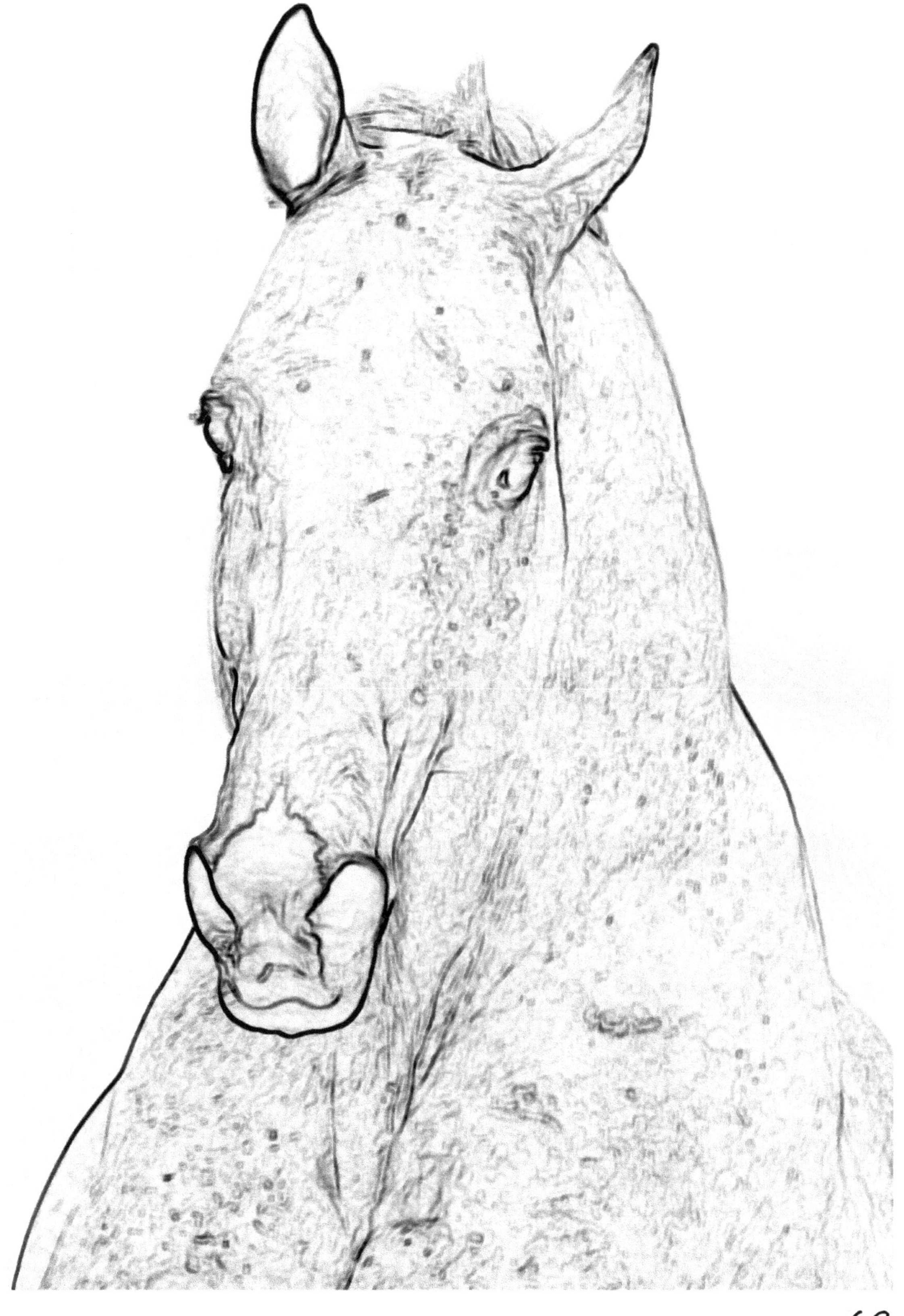

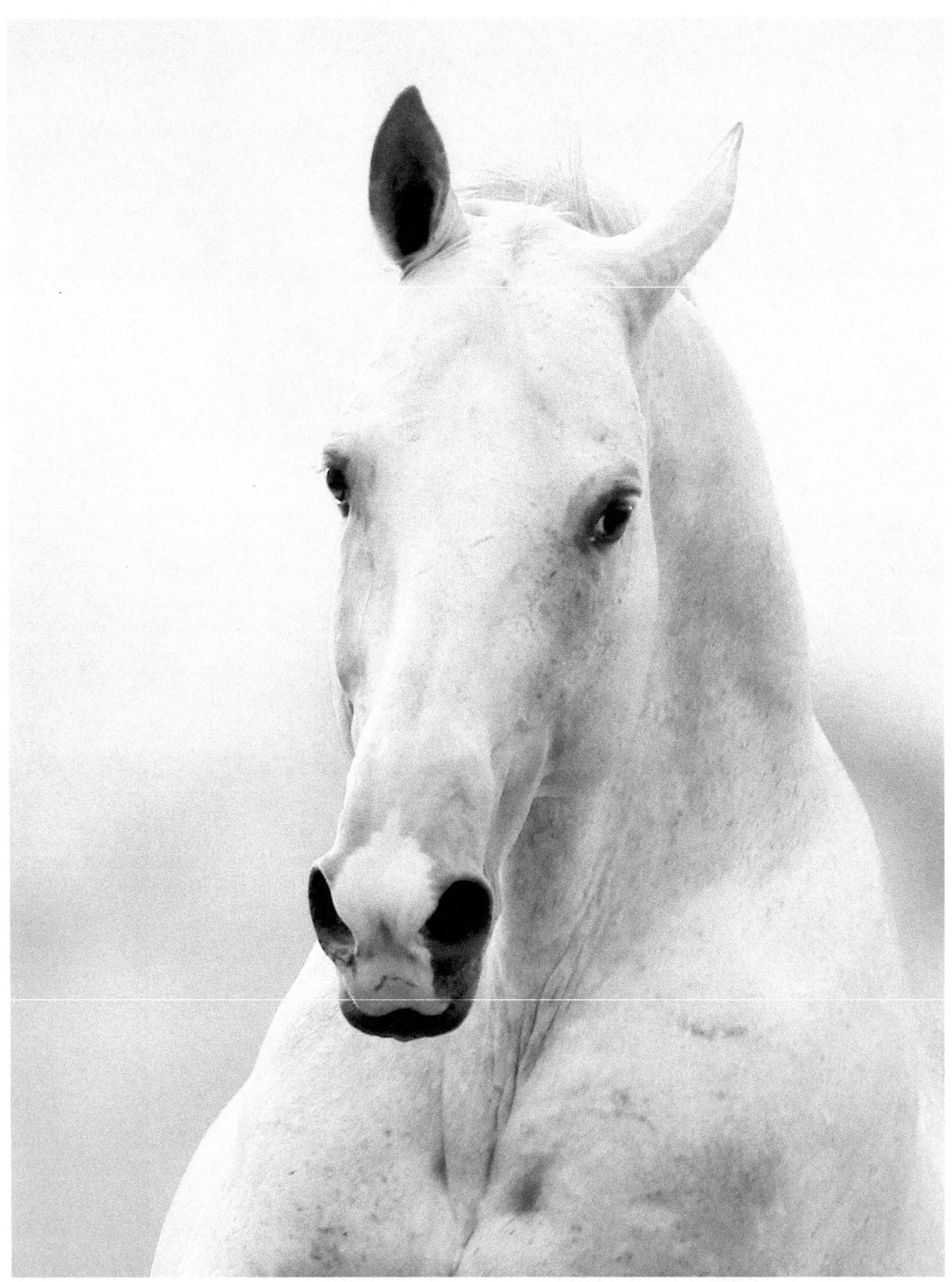

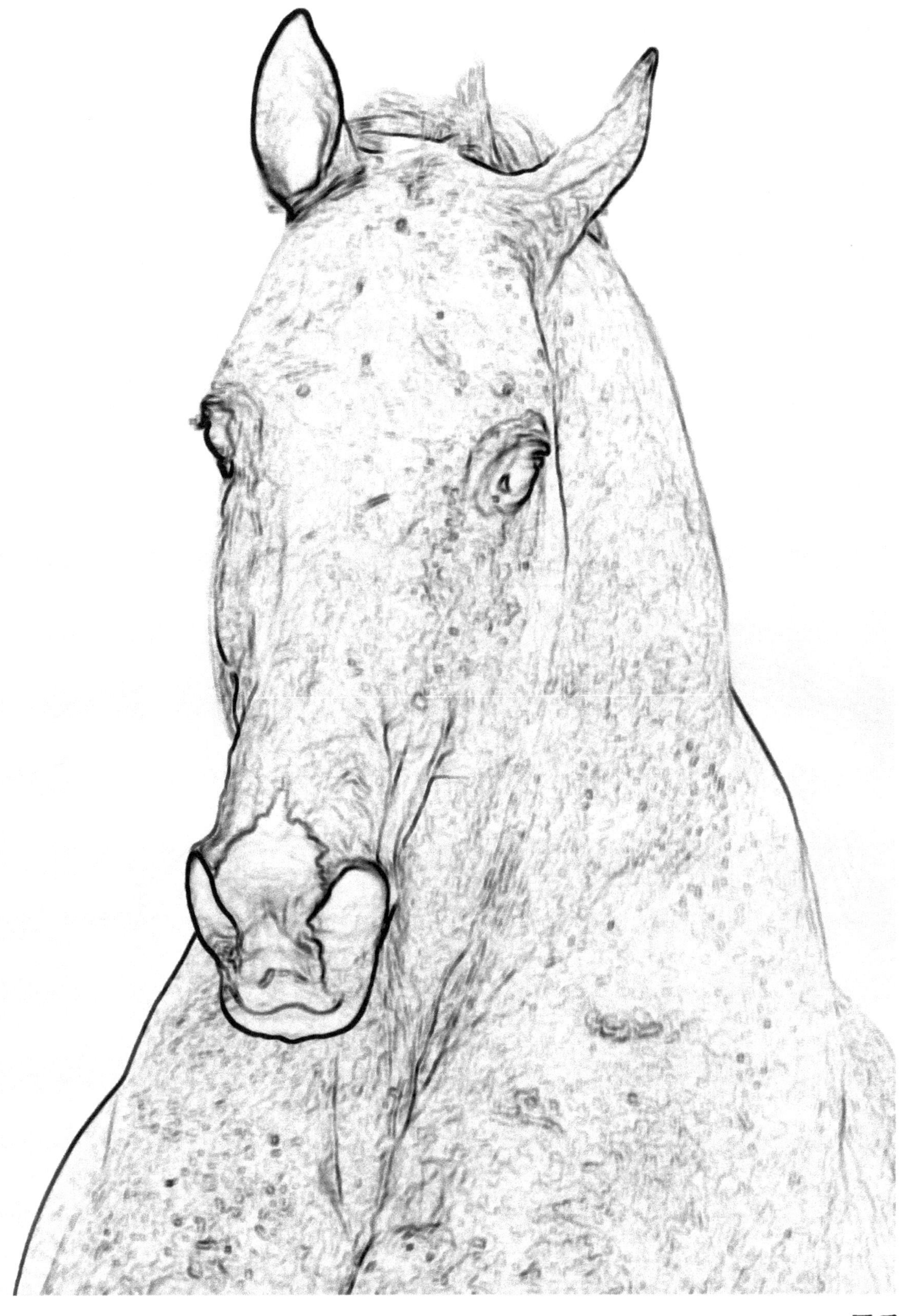

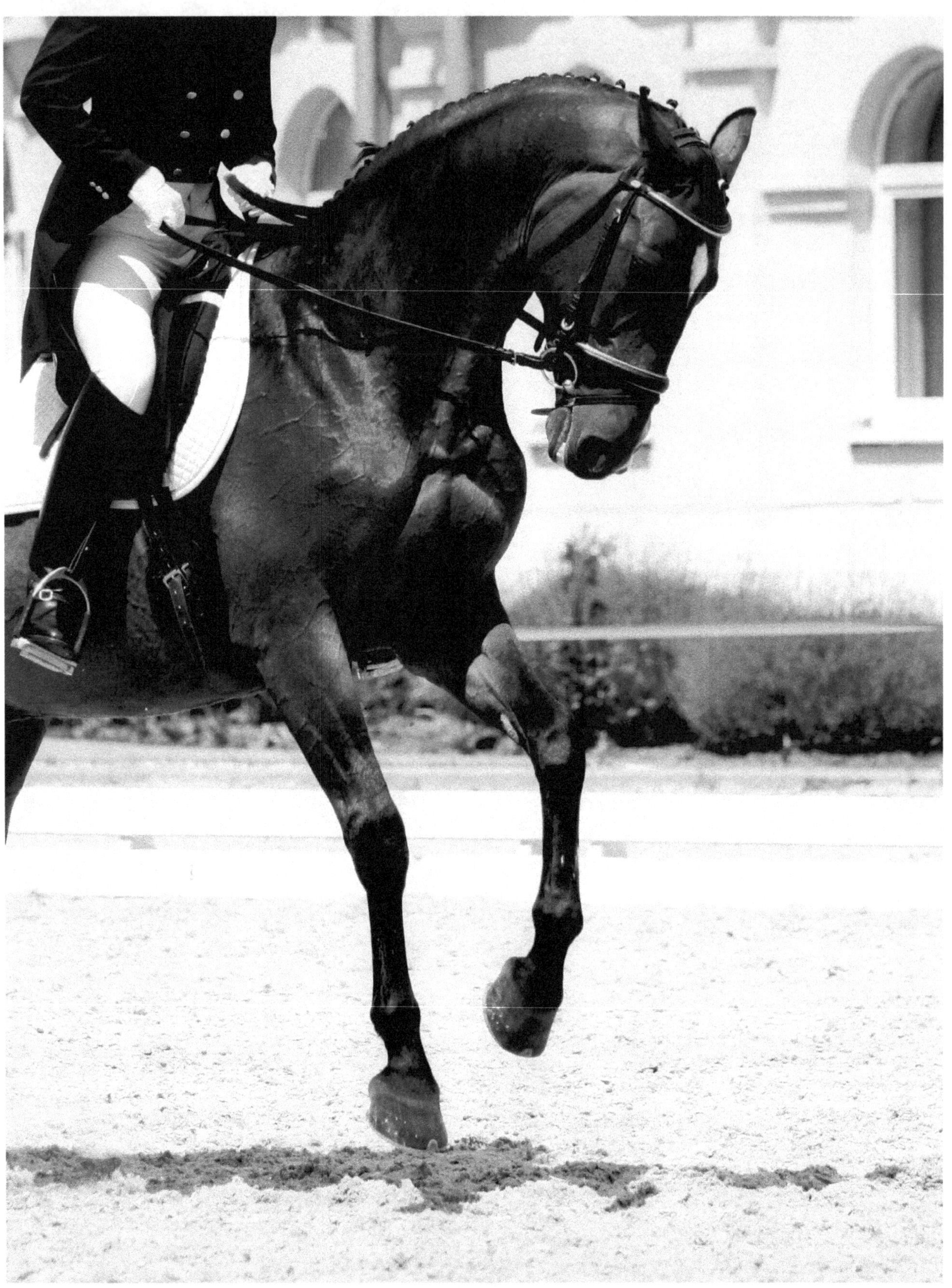

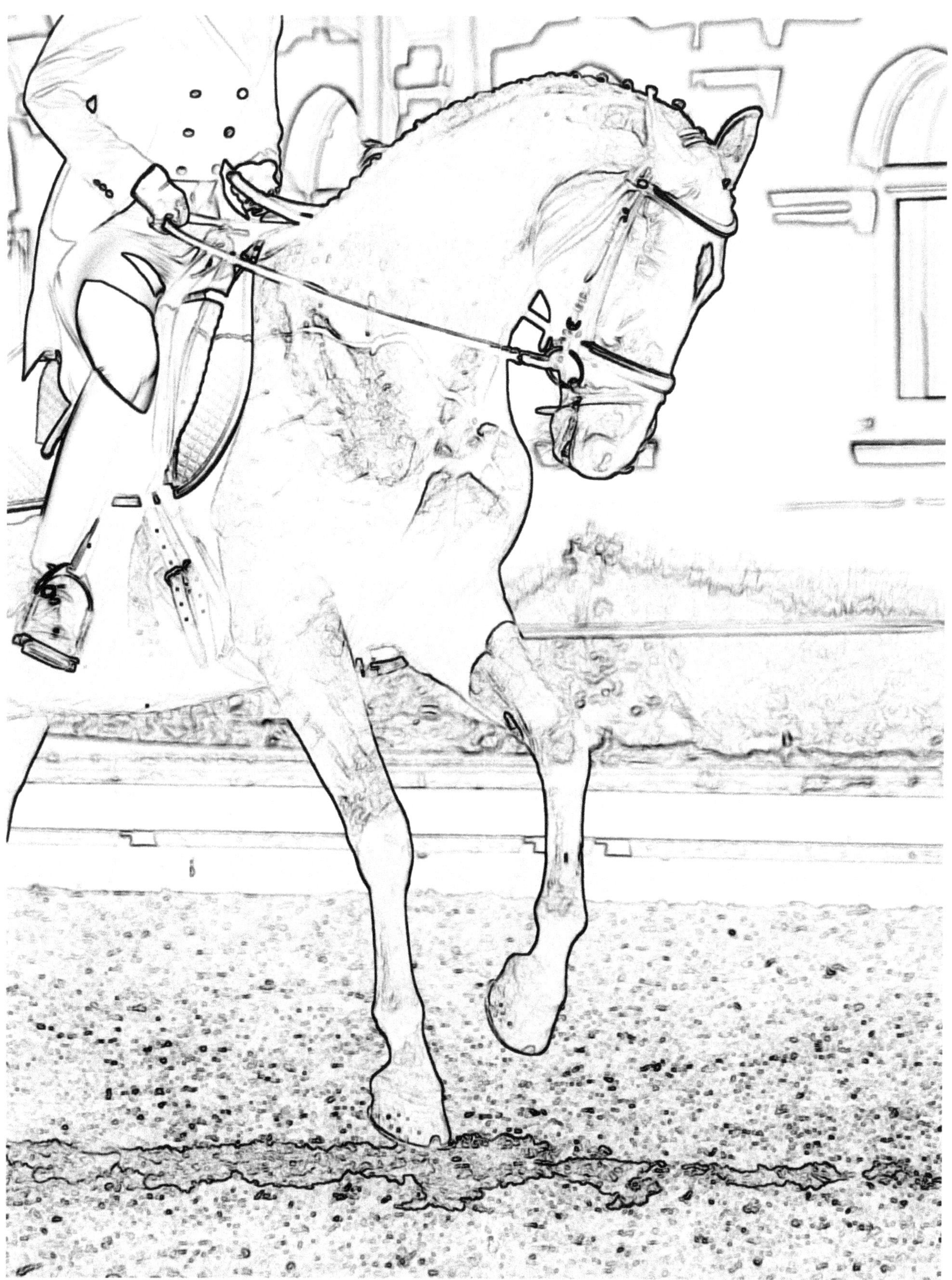

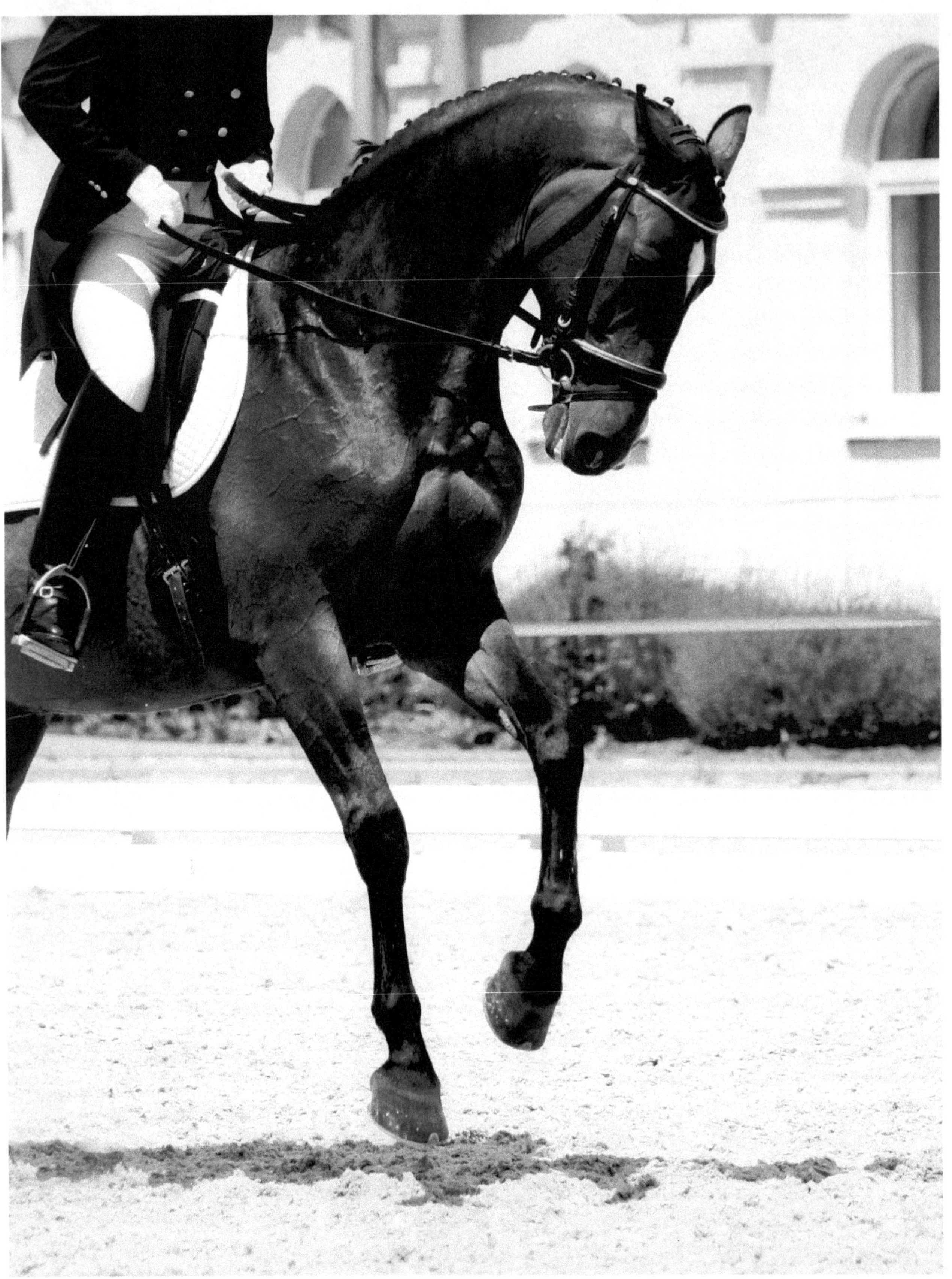

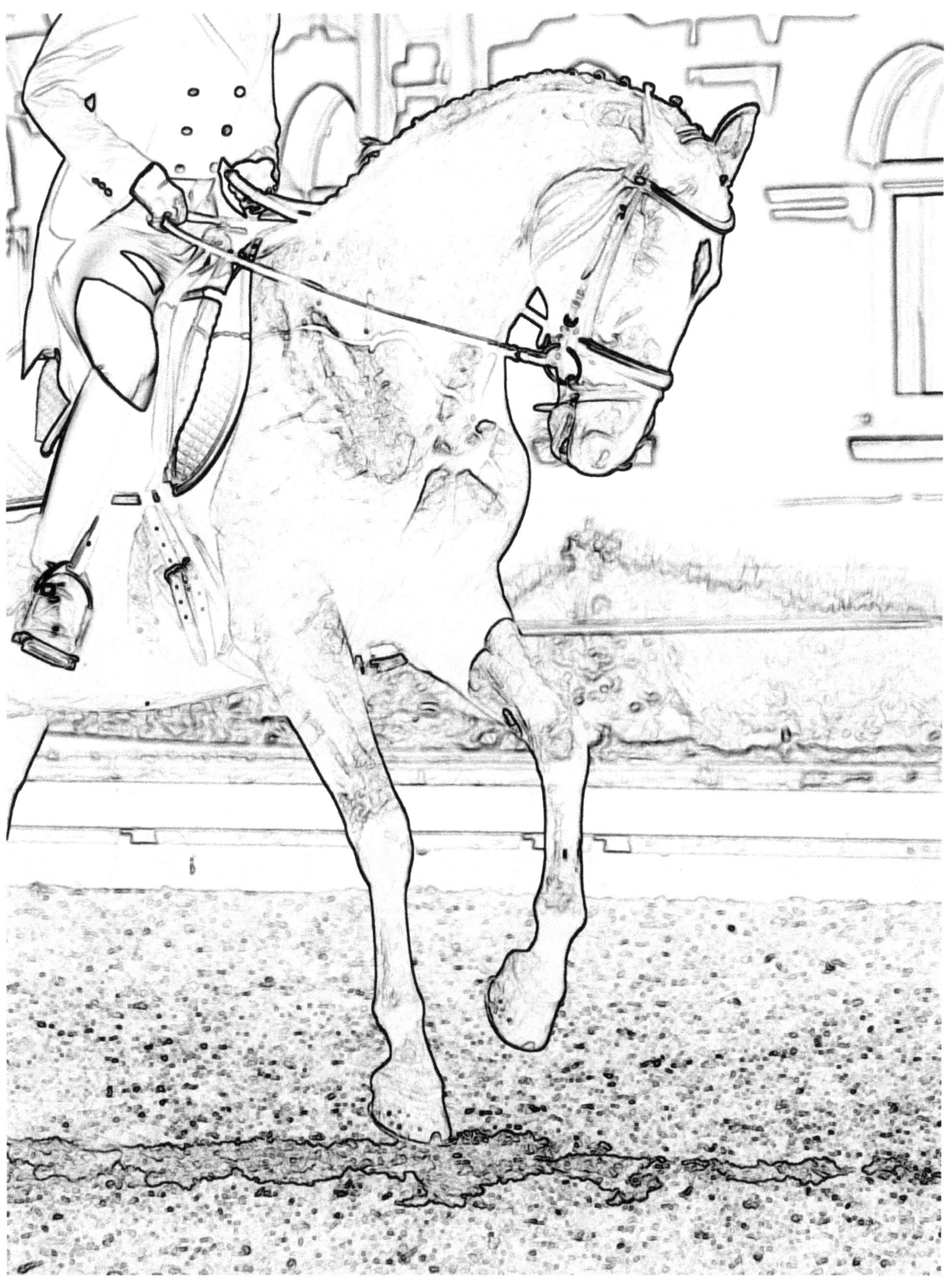

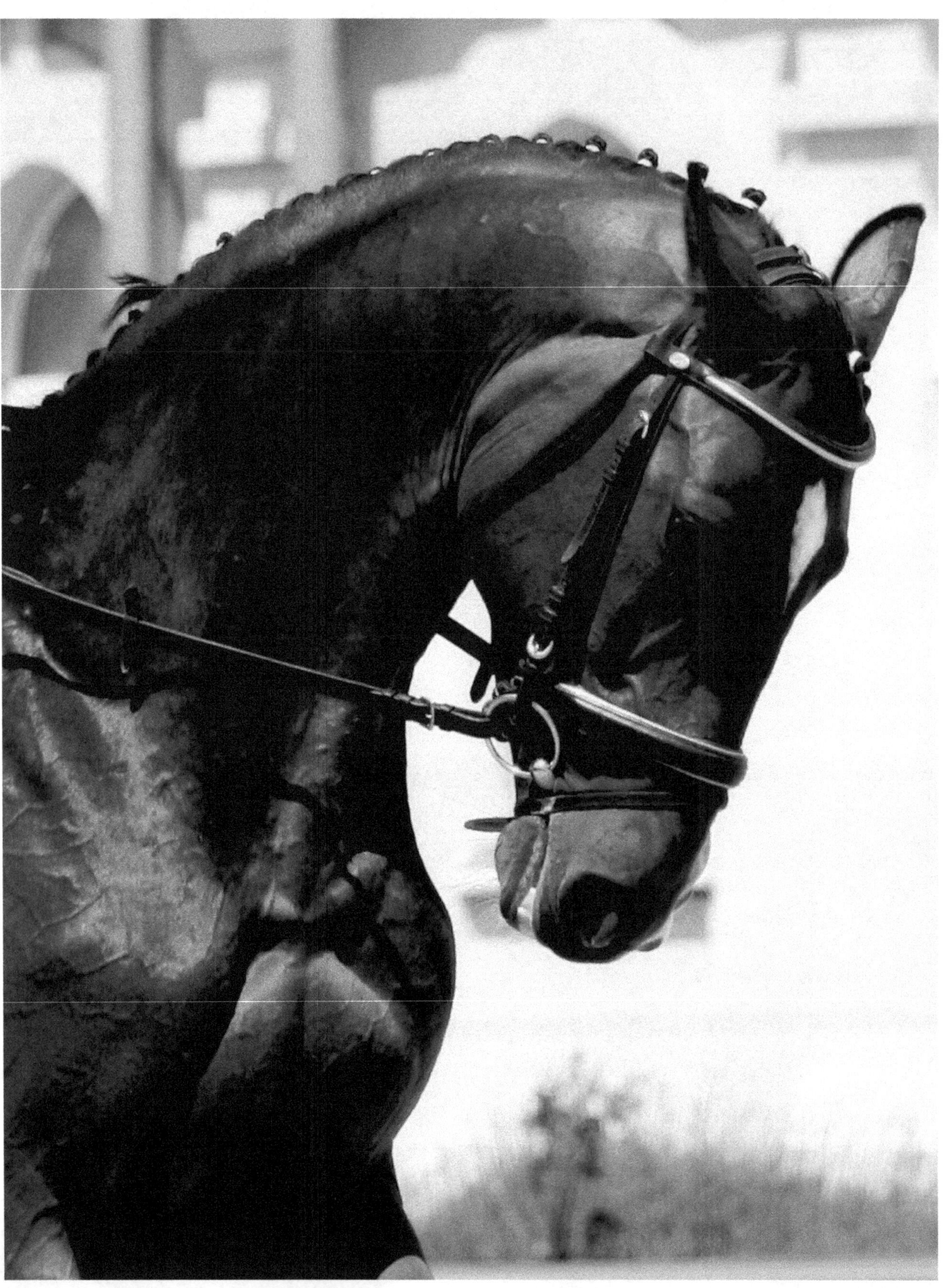

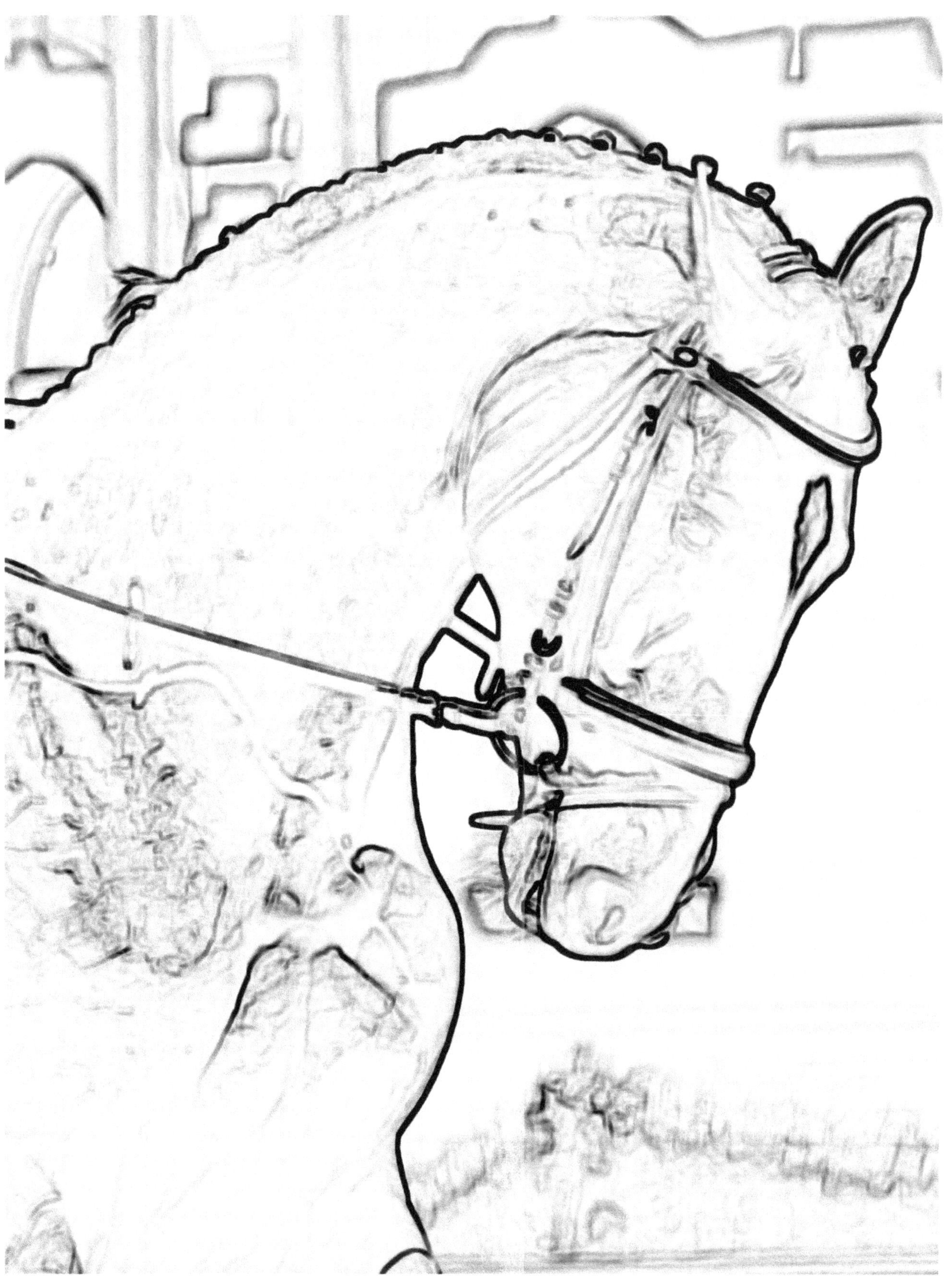

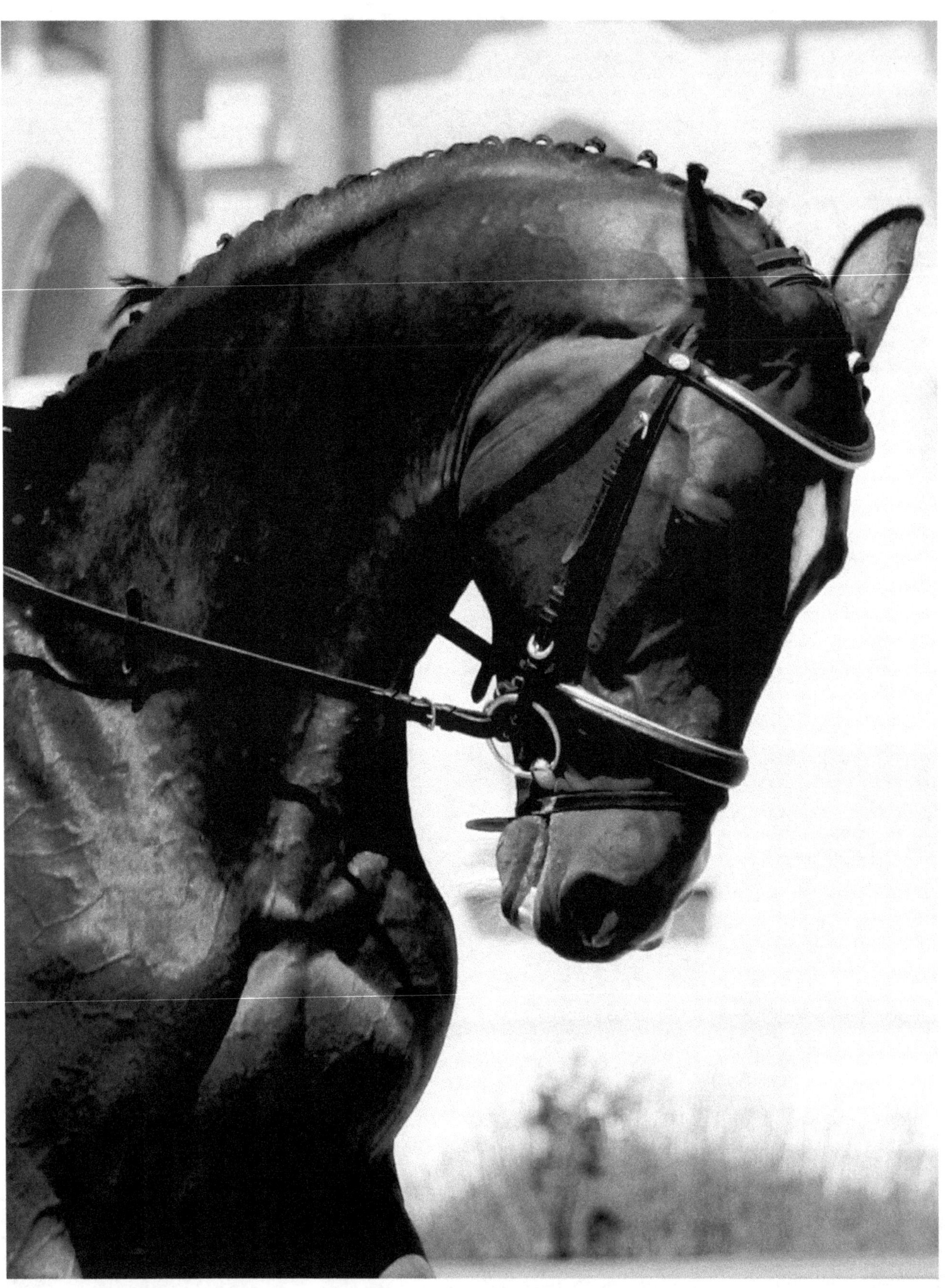

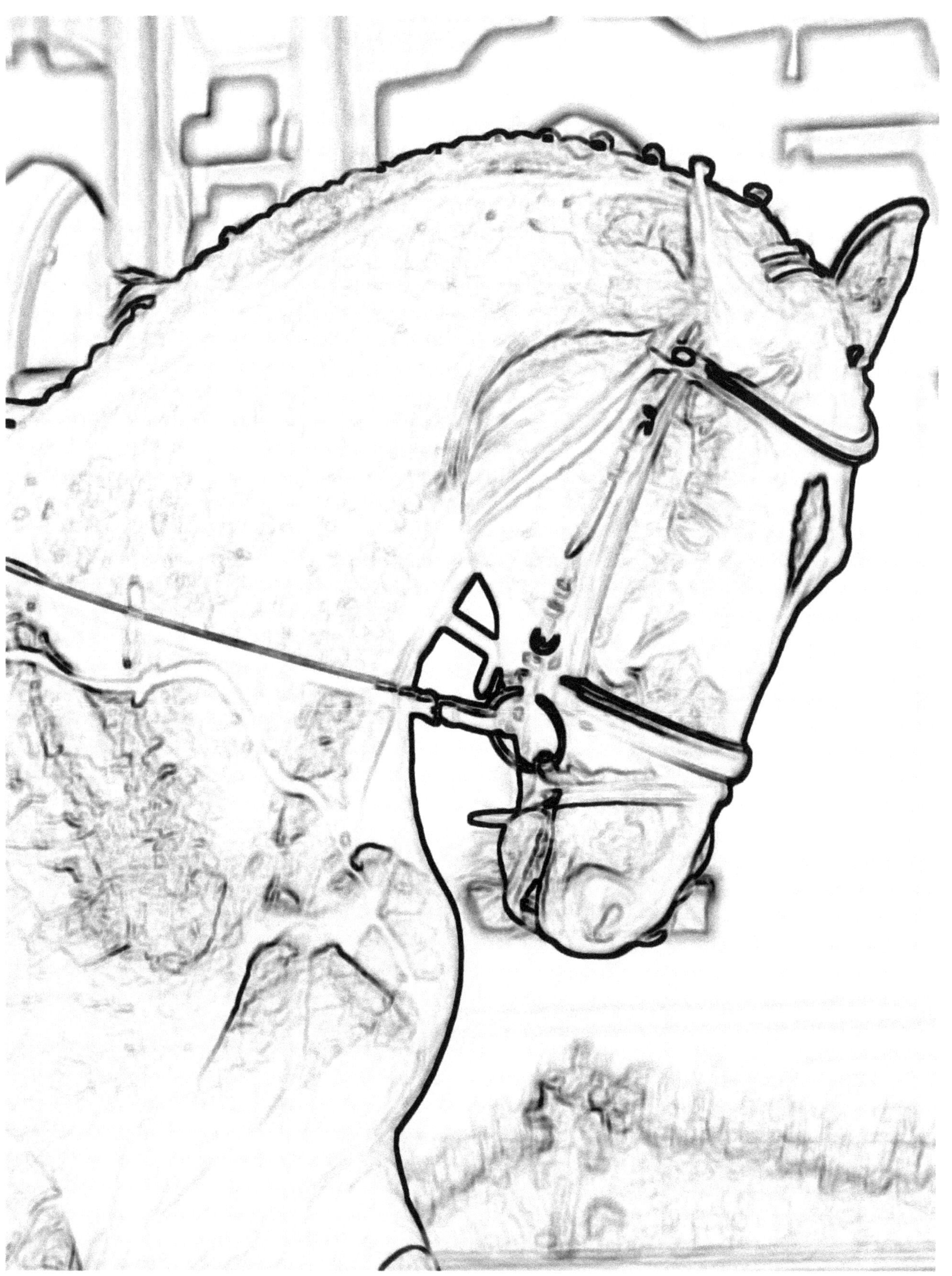

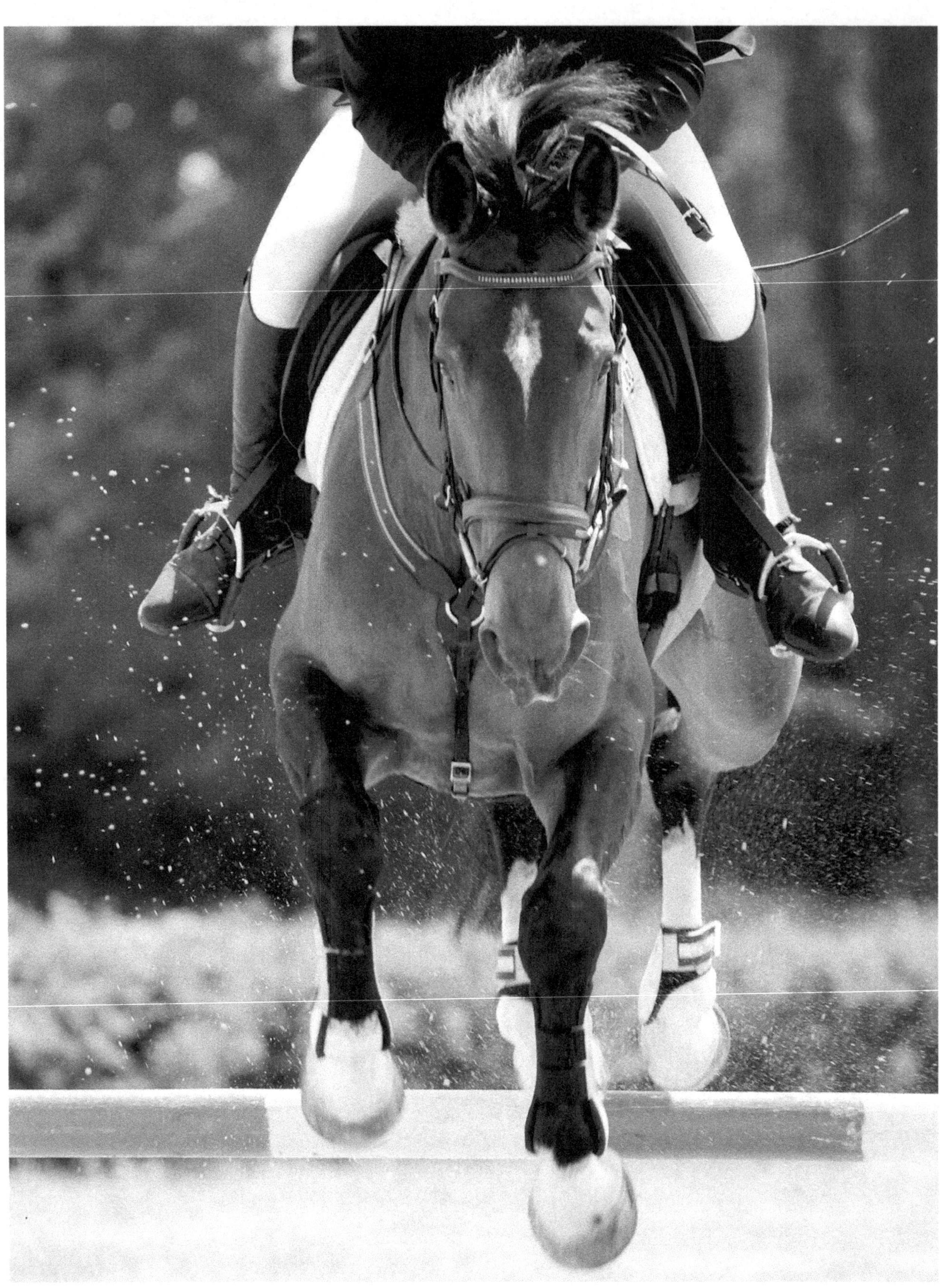

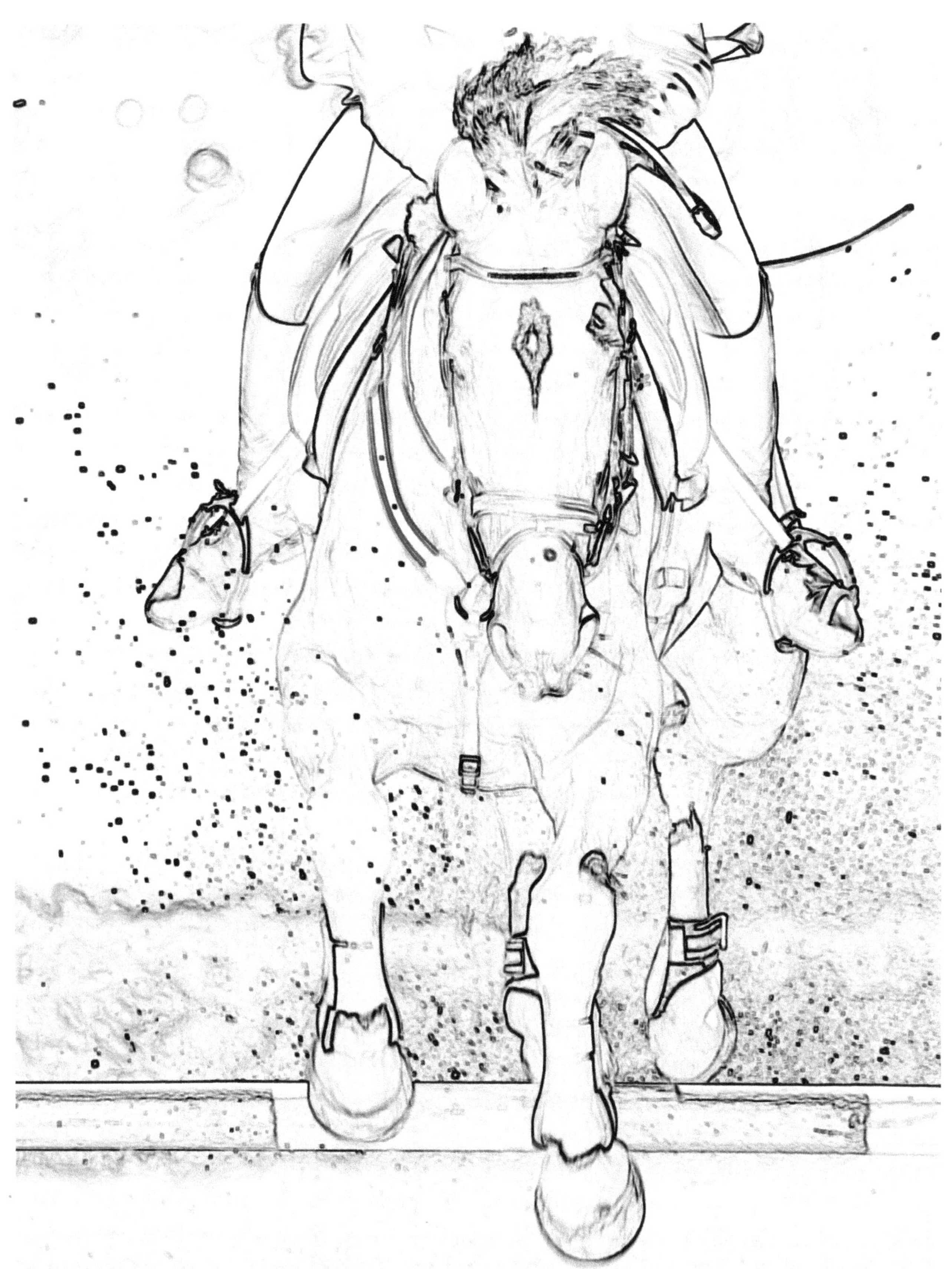

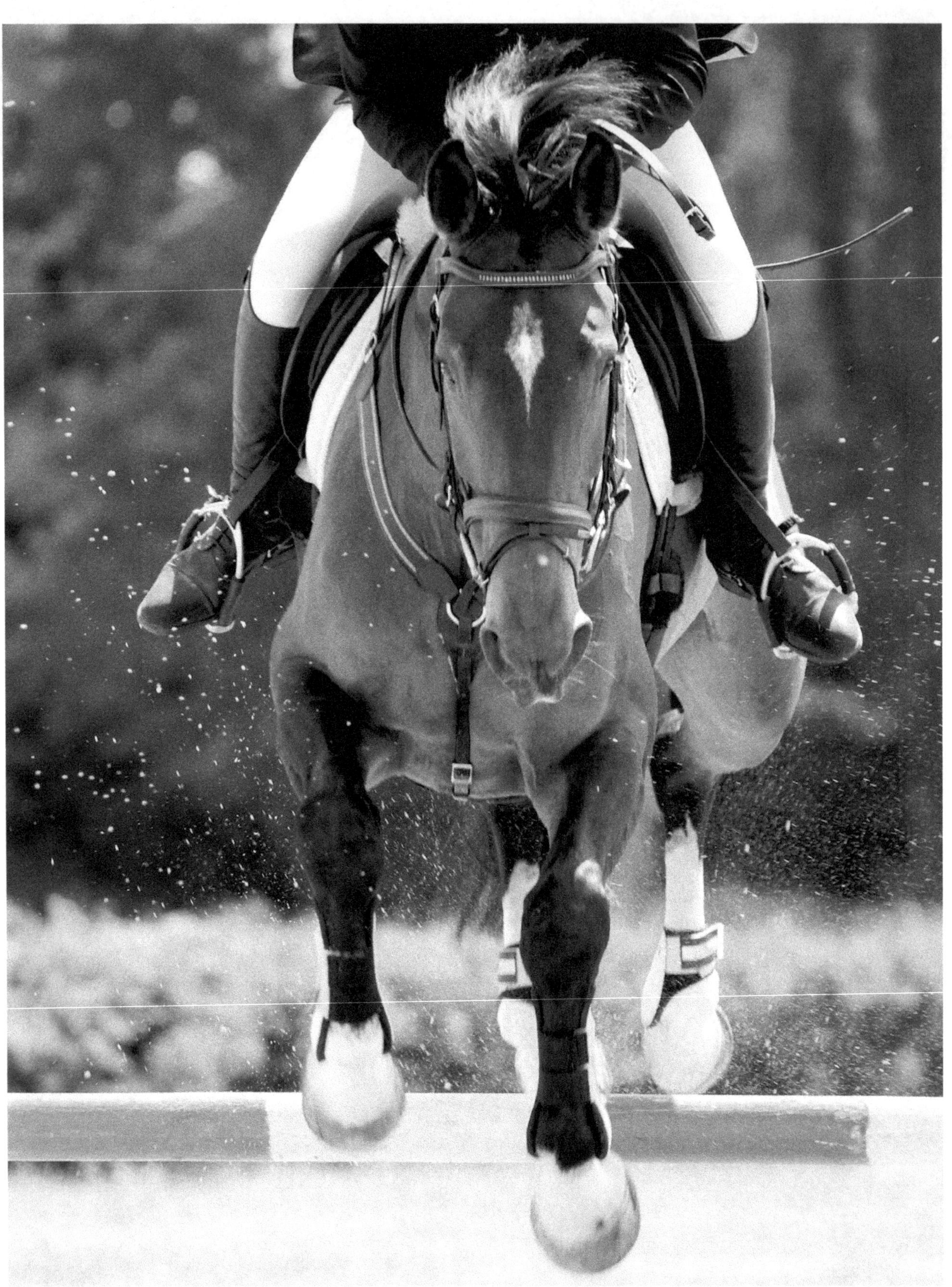

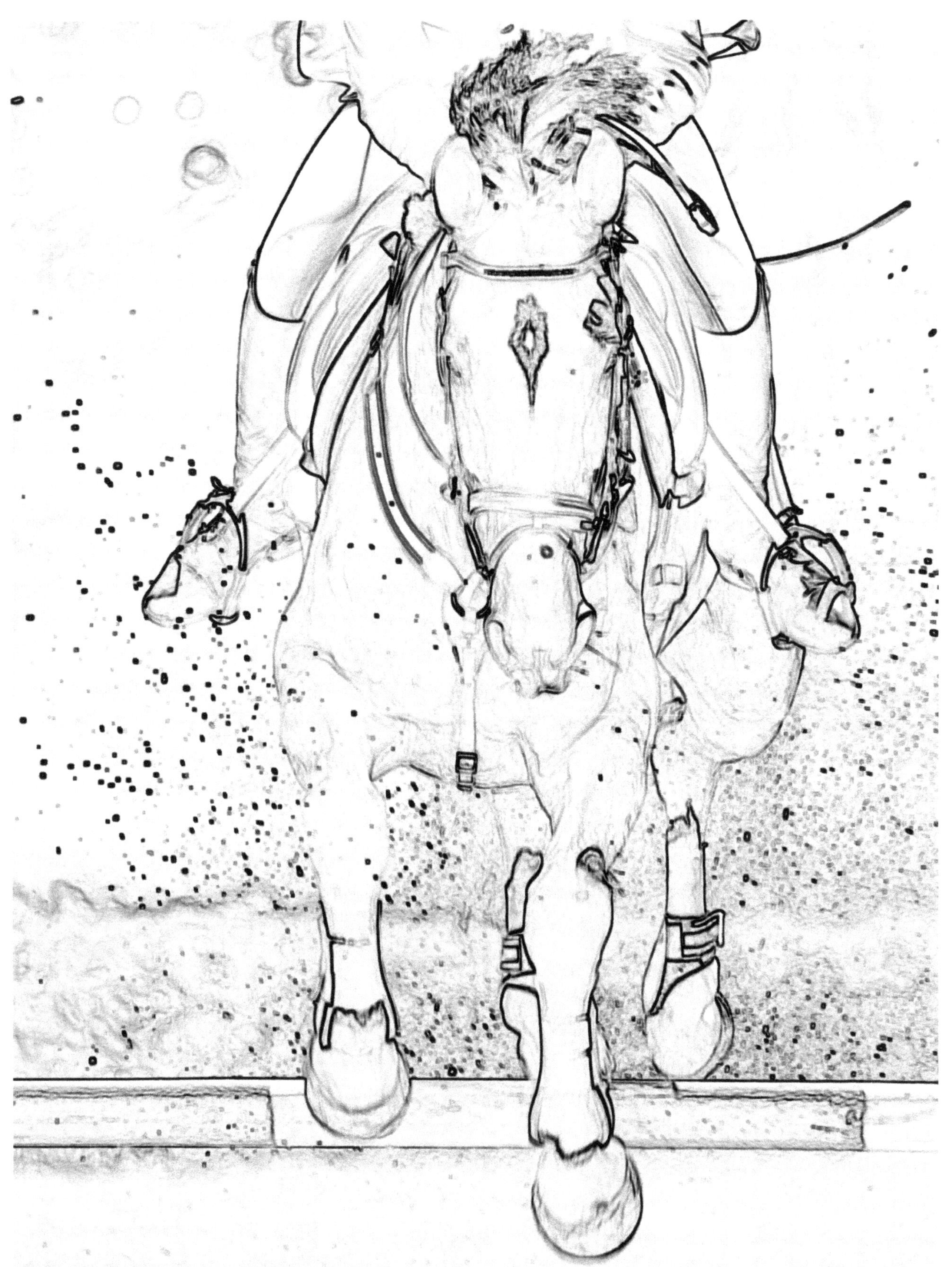

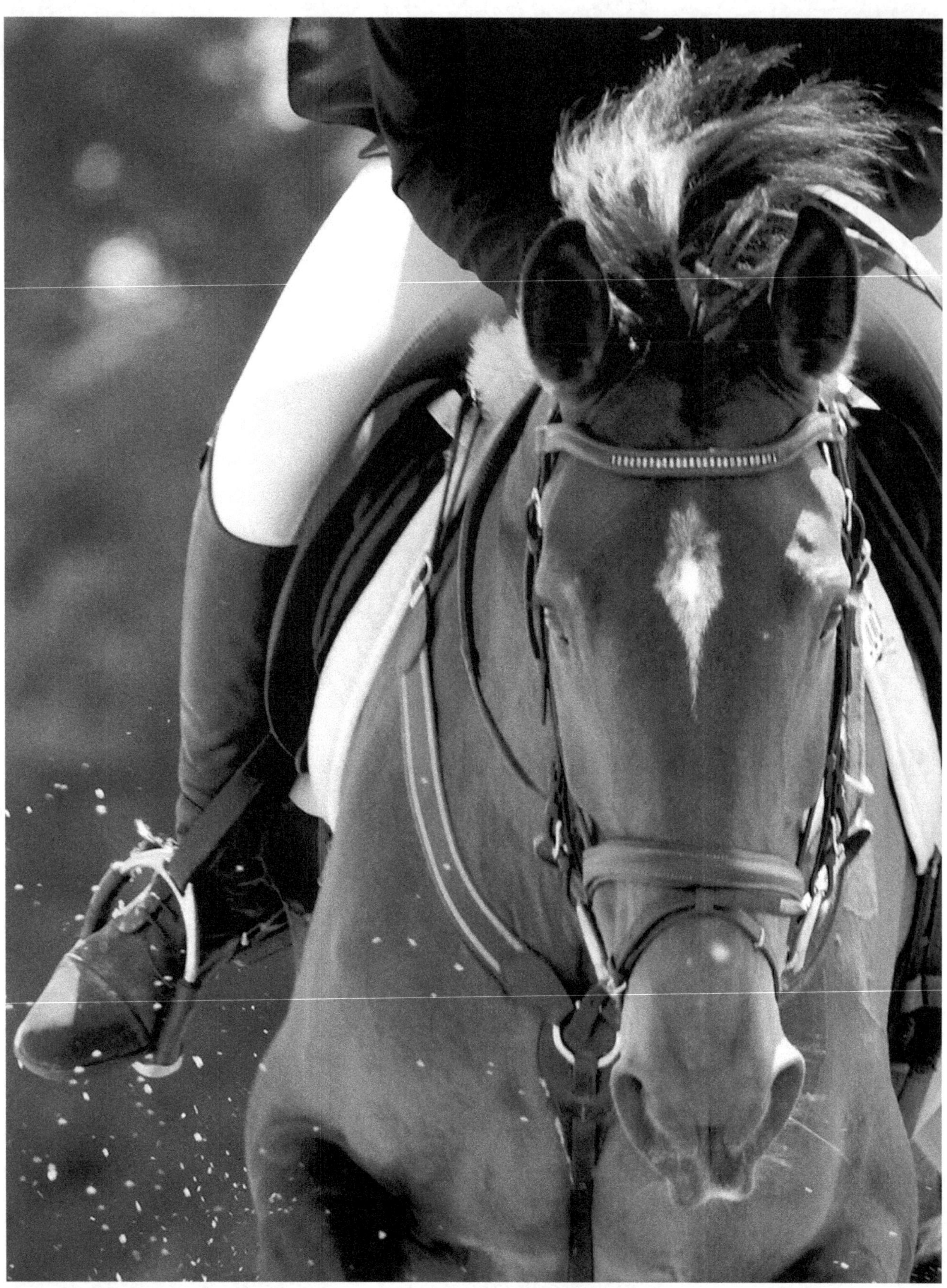

 Practice Drawing XL 11: Horses

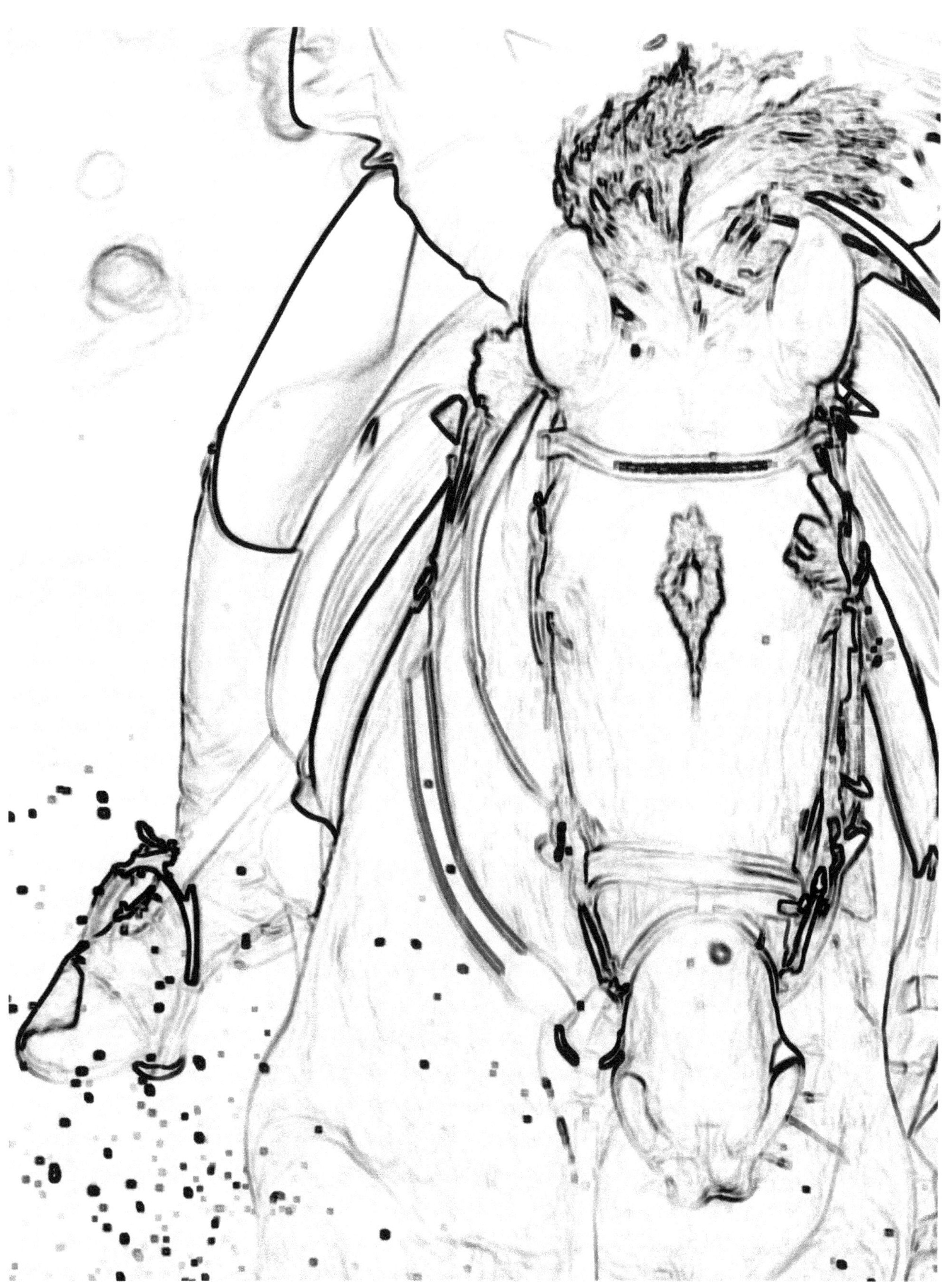

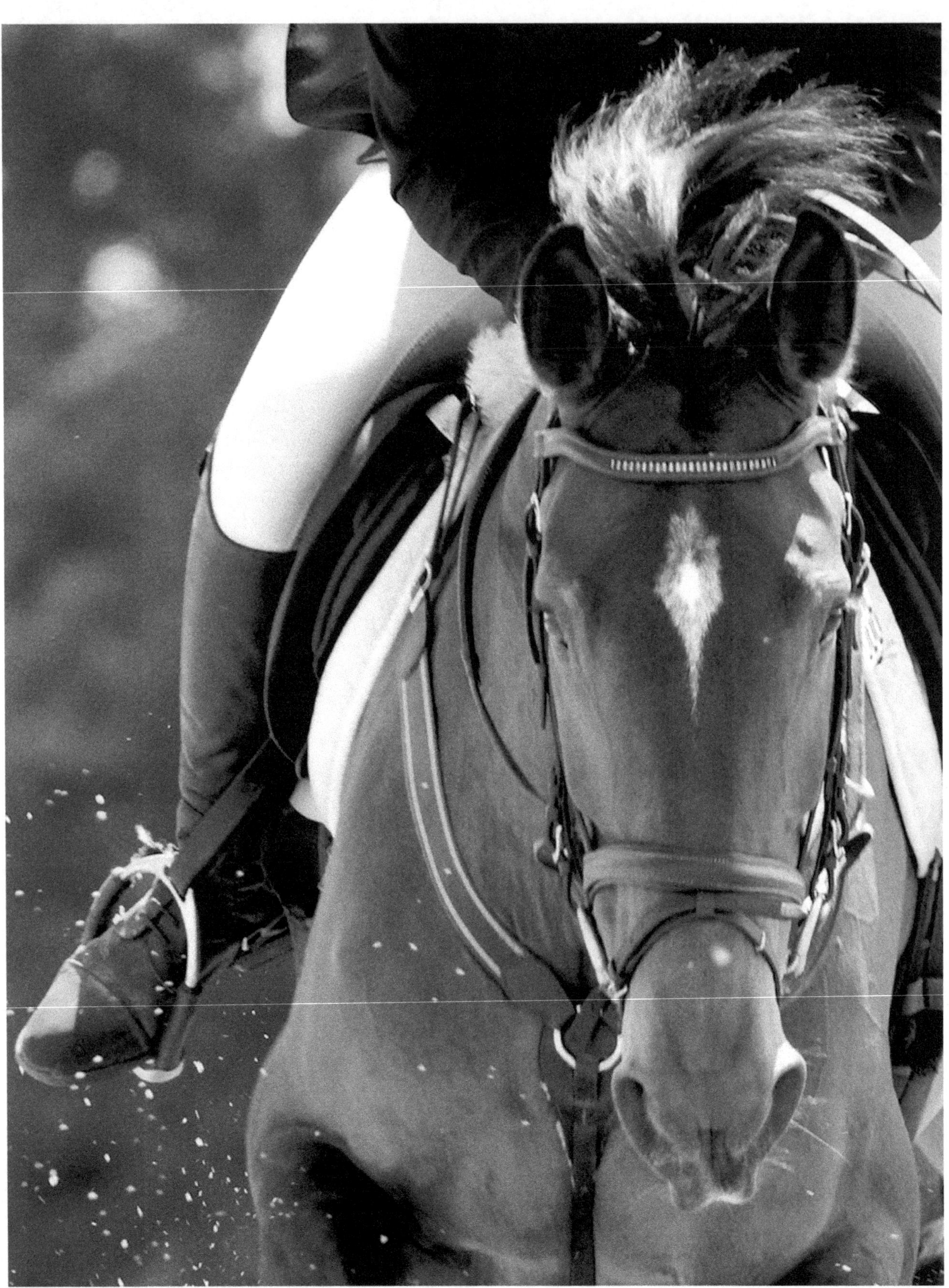

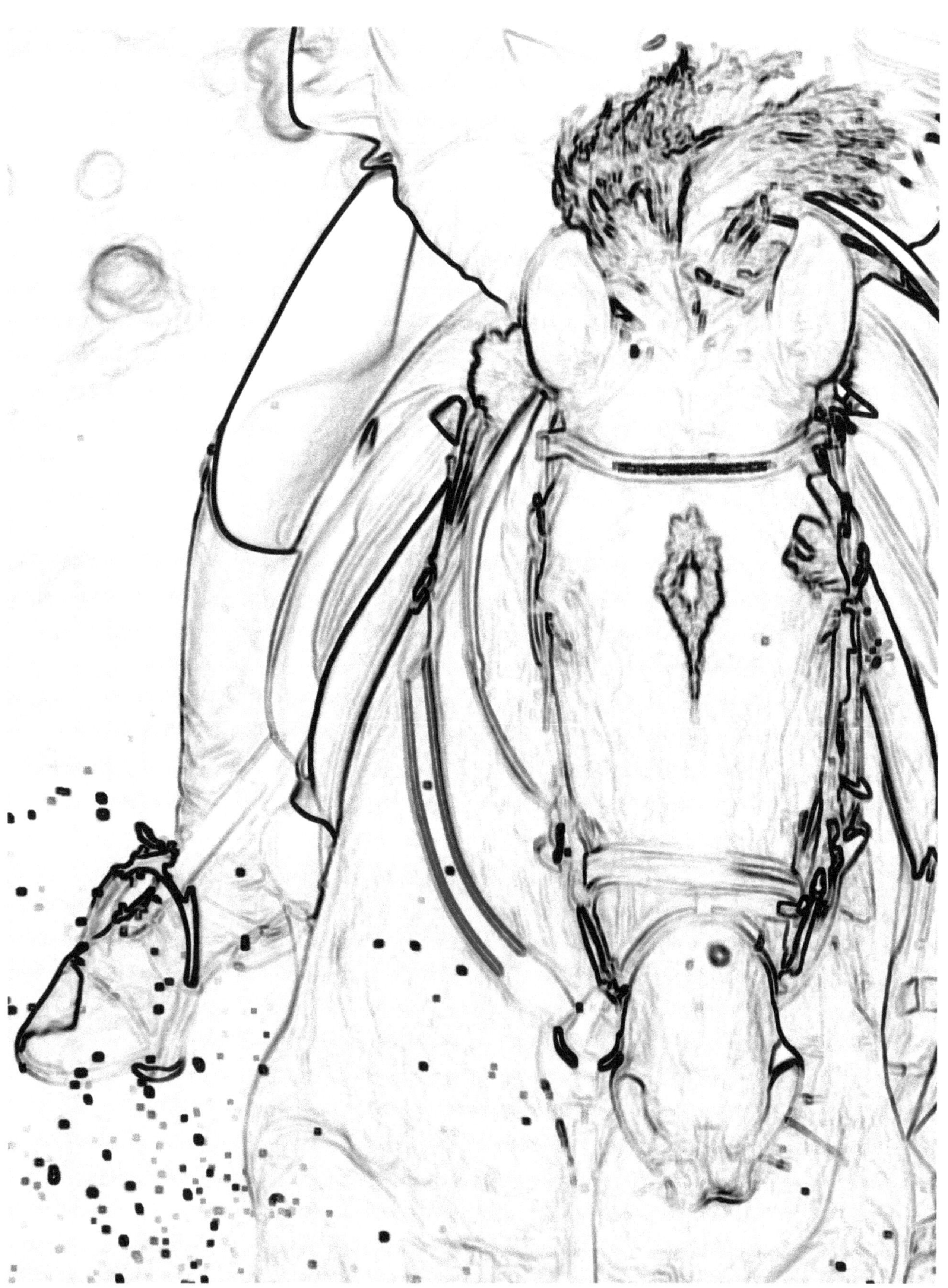

York P. Herpers Practice Drawing
XL Workbook 14: Flowers
HERPERS Publishing International
York P. Herpers Practice Drawing
XL Workbook 25: Buddha
HERPERS Publishing International
York P. Herpers Practice Drawing
XL Workbook 4: Female Nude
HERPERS Publishing International
York P. Herpers Practice Drawing
XL Workbook 13: Sports Car
HERPERS Publishing International

www.ingramcontent.com/pod-product-compliance
Lightning Source LLC
Chambersburg PA
CBHW082107110425
24991CB00037B/1406